I0439848

U.S. ARMY

2014 ARMY EQUIPMENT MODERNIZATION PLAN

13 May 2013

Page Left Blank

TABLE OF CONTENTS

EXECUTIVE SUMMARY

The Army Equipment Modernization Plan 2014 describes the Army Research, Development, and Acquisition (RDA) for ten capability portfolio areas and the Science and Technology portion of Fiscal Year 2014 (FY 14) President's Budget Request. The plan breaks down the RDA investments into ten capability portfolio areas, highlights the portfolio accomplishments over the last two years and provides intent for FY 14 investments as well as the way ahead. Dollars and quantities in this document do not reflect sequestration impacts.

In addition to capability portfolio investment strategies, the plan links RDA investments to Army Strategy and discusses specific modernization priorities and objectives, priority materiel programs, the Army's Science and Technology program, equipment fielding and distribution.

The Soldier and Squad are the foundation of our Army. Army equipment modernization builds from the Soldier out, equipping our Squads for tactical overmatch in all situations, connected to an integrated network, and operating in vehicles that improve mobility and lethality while preserving survivability.

The objective of Army equipment modernization is to develop and field versatile and tailorable equipment that is affordable, sustainable, cost-effective, enables our Soldiers to fight and win across the entire range of conflict. To achieve this objective the Army uses portfolio management to help ensure efficiencies and eliminate redundancies, evolutionary acquisition to ensure program risk is reduced by emphasizing mature technologies, and the Army readiness model to ensure the timely fielding of equipment.

The Army will continue to pursue mission command capabilities by enhancing our network; remain prepared for decisive action by improving or transforming our combat platforms; and enable Soldiers and squads with improved lethality, protection and situational awareness. These enhancements also enable our Soldiers and squads to leverage Joint capabilities.

As the Army transitions from Afghanistan and reinforces its commitment in the Asia-pacific region, the Army will continue to make cost-effective, sustainable and affordable choices. Overall, our modernization efforts will prepare the total force for a complex and uncertain battlefield by putting squads, with precise information and overmatch capability, in the right place at the right time to accomplish their mission. This plan enhances our advantages leader development, mobility, logistics at the tactical, operational, and strategic levels of our Army, and C4I.

Details on major Army acquisition programs can be found in the
2013 Army Weapon Systems handbook at:
http://armyalt.va.newsmemory.com/wsh.php

Linking Resource Decisions to Army Strategy

LINKING RESOURCE DECISIONS TO ARMY STRATEGY

We face a complex and interconnected global operational environment with a range of threats, challenges and opportunities. This makes it likely that U.S. forces will be called on to conduct operations in any of a broad range of conditions. At the same time, innovation in technology and changes across the political landscape are reshaping the strategic environment, multiplying and improving the capabilities actors are able to obtain. Additionally, the fiscal environment is a key factor that will impact our national defense for decades to come.

The Army has a key role in the shaping of the strategic environment and in the execution of the majority of operations the armed forces will be required to conduct. Among the capabilities provided to the combatant commanders, the Army builds and operates the space and terrestrial communication networks that connect our own units, the Joint community, and interagency and multinational partners. Soldiers provide essential logistics infrastructure, delivering food, fuel, ammunition, materiel and medical support that sustain Joint operations ranging from combat to humanitarian assistance. In addition, the Army collects and analyzes the intelligence that informs our actions and measures our progress, and provides the majority of the forces in U.S. Special Operations Command.

The 2014 Army Equipment Modernization Plan addresses the strategic, technological and fiscal environments as the Army adjusts following a decade of intense conflict and moves to a broader Joint mission focus and our priorities and investments to equip the Army.

THE STRATEGIC ENVIRONMENT

Entering into our 12th consecutive year of war, Afghanistan remains our top priority. We continue to ensure that our Soldiers deployed are fully trained, equipped, and ready. As we equip the Force to carry out current operations and continue to reset our returning forces, we also prepare for future operations. Our goal is to ensure we are prepared even in an uncertain future. To do this, we must widen our aperture for broad Joint mission sets, across varied geographies, and during a time of declining budgets. This Army Equipment Modernization Plan is the stepping off point that addresses current needs and supports the Army Equipment Modernization Strategy that will help us determine which systems to procure, which technologies to invest in, and which applications to integrate during the yearly budgeting process.

In an increasingly interconnected world, the Army plays a critical role in shaping the strategic environment. Our Total Force has honed its tremendous skills not only in battle, but also quelling civil unrest, countering terrorism, demilitarizing former combat zones, protecting vulnerable populations, and providing disaster relief. They include building partnerships through standing organizations such as Joint Task Force Bravo in Central America since 1984 and Combined Joint Task Force-Horn of Africa since 2002.

The Army is an indispensable provider to the Joint Force, and we will continue that role with a smaller, more agile Army. Army Commanders lead Joint Task Forces, plan operations, and command and control units across the range of military operations. Army

---

units build and operate the networks connecting our own units, the Joint community, interagency, and multinational partners on austere battlefields.

Soldiers deliver food, fuel, ammunition, and medical support necessary to sustain joint operations from combat to humanitarian assistance. The Army collects and analyzes the intelligence that informs our actions and measures our progress. It delivers vital supplies to communities, at home and abroad, impacted by natural disasters. And finally, the Army provides 75 percent of the operators in U.S. Special Operations Command, who are essential to our national counter-terrorism and security force assistance operations.

The strategic environment will remain complex. The interaction of many variables within the environment, including human behavior, assures both fog and friction as adversaries continue to search for, find, and exploit vulnerabilities through increasingly sophisticated technologies. The current strategic environment is more ambiguous than past decades, presenting multiple layers of complexity and challenging the Army with threats beyond traditional warfighting skills and training. This complexity extends beyond the battlefield and throughout all levels of the Army's supply chain as resource; energy and water scarcity will increasingly constrain our options, create exploitable vulnerabilities, and reduce access to key commodities and affordable materiel solutions. As we remain committed to responsibly ending the current fight in Afghanistan, we will reinforce our posture to respond to contingencies in the Pacific, Middle East, and other regions around the world.

To truly become a force capable of engaging around the world and to provide credible deterrence requires an equipment modernization plan that is centered on our Soldiers and squad. We must empower them with unmatched lethality, protection, and situational awareness to achieve

tactical dominance. It entails an overarching network architecture that connects all echelons –from the squad through the Joint Task Force to the Enterprise and home station - to ensure leaders have the most complete information possible at the right time to make the best possible decisions. It includes network-ready combat and tactical wheeled vehicles designed to maneuver our formations with increased lethality and mobility, while optimizing for force protection, sustainability and survivability. Our modernization efforts will prepare the Total Force for the complex and uncertain battlefield by putting squads with access to necessary information, with overmatch capability at the decisive time and place to dominate in the operational environment. At the same time, we must preserve the ability to reassemble our Forces rapidly, building the mass necessary to decisively defeat a determined enemy. In pursuing these goals, we ensure that we remain an Army capable of many missions, at many speeds, under many conditions.

To build and maintain these fundamental capabilities, we must make affordable, sustainable, and cost-effective decisions which simultaneously accomplish several key tasks: 1) provide joint commanders versatile and tailorable capabilities; 2) maintain the capacity to deter and defeat future adversaries; and 3) integrate rapidly evolving technologies to avoid block obsolescence of our platforms and systems, while searching for future disruptive technologies. Our approach is to integrate mature technologies and incremental improvements while investing in military-unique technologies for the future.

To do this, the Army is expanding its planning horizon to encompass the near-term (out to six years) to the far-term (beyond 30 years). This long range planning will facilitate knowledge points, enabling decision points for considering equipment age, degradation of overmatch abilities, industrial base viability (economic, political, environmental, and resource considerations), and closure of capability gaps in a near, mid, and far-term timeframes, while also allowing for cost-informed decisions. Although we do not have a specific threat or location to focus on, we do know that the future environment will require versatile and tailorable formations with fundamental capabilities that are ready for rapid and scalable global employment to meet combatant commander's needs for land forces in support of the National Defense Strategy.

The reality is that capability gaps will emerge and disappear rapidly -- military requirements will not remain constant so our Requirement, Resource, Acquisition and Sustainment processes must adjust to remain agile.

- Our equipment and acquisition must be versatile: Just as our forces are regionally aligned and mission tailored, our equipment must be adaptable to geographic requirements. Given the diversity of the 11 defense missions, our equipment must work safely in various terrains, in cold and hot weather, and in energy and water constrained environments. We must retain the capability to quickly procure equipment based on changing mission needs, which is an Army priority, but make tough decisions on when it is cost-effective to do so.

- Our equipment modernization efforts must consider Joint, Interagency, Intergovernmental and Multinational (JIIM) and Coalition interoperability: Interoperability and interdependence will become increasingly important with reductions in U.S. force structure; globally integrated operations will leverage unique capabilities of each military Service and Coalition partner.

- Our equipment must support tailorable formations: Combatant commanders will utilize Army formations from the individual Soldier through Corps; therefore, our equipment and systems have to be scalable to different sized formations and retain capacity to surge quantities to meet mobilization needs.

- We must retain the ability to deter and defeat adversaries: Modernization preserves the Army's core capability to prepare for future challenges.

- Our combat enablers will remain in high demand: Army capabilities such as engineers, military intelligence, air defense, aviation, communication, logistics and military police will maintain a high operational deployment tempo; keeping them resilient and equipped with up-to-date technologies is a priority.

- We must reduce the training, maintaining, safety and health issues, energy, and water burdens to use equipment: Since we cannot anticipate which formations will deploy where, equipment that is "intuitive" in use, energy and water efficient/flexible, will greatly increase our versatility; human factors engineering and virtual simulation-based training are highly desired attributes. This also supports the Army's goal to improve energy efficiency and reflects our changing culture that makes power and energy a consideration in everything we do.

THE TECHNOLOGICAL ENVIRONMENT

In the past, we were able to anticipate capability gaps based upon a relatively static threat, but that model has disintegrated over the past two decades. Today, non-state actors and other nations are capable of acquiring advanced communications, cyber, unmanned aviation, and weapons that provide them sophisticated capabilities. Additionally, the commercial sector in many industries has grown much larger than the traditional defense sector causing a disconnect in the rate of innovation between commercial-technologies and military-technologies. The effect of this disconnect is that we must change how we think about our traditional weapon systems and disaggregate them into three pieces to take advantage of commercial advances and mitigate potential vulnerabilities:

- Components: These are items for which technologies rapidly change (three to five year cycles) such as sensors, software, and communication equipment; we want them to be adaptable and reconfigurable across multiple platforms, expansible (readily updated in response to changing circumstances) and linked together to close multiple capability gaps; innovation is primarily driven by commercially available technologies requiring the Army to maintain and improve a core ability to integrate components across multiple systems and sub-systems; these components must be built with the understanding that size, weight and power must be minimized.

- Sub-Systems: These are the devices that link components to our platforms, for which technology changes more slowly (once a decade) such as engines, gun tubes, radios, and cockpits; they enable our platforms to shoot, move, and communicate; innovation is shared between the commercial and defense sectors, requiring careful integration of investments in areas such as encryption, robotics, unmanned systems, networking/energy efficiency, energetic materials and mobility.

- Systems: Systems host our component and sub-systems, for which technology changes very slowly (several decades) such as tanks, helicopters, watercraft, and facilities; there are generally fewer commercial innovations, forcing us to rely on government funded research efforts in areas such as protection, survivability and lethality; replacing systems is often expensive and takes a generation; some of our systems need to be replaced in the near-term as the threat has made them obsolete, while others will be with us for many decades.

THE FISCAL ENVIRONMENT

As a Nation, we are living in the midst of both a global and national fiscal crisis. The near-term is forcing crucial decisions relating to structure, readiness, and equipment modernization. Decisions made in the next few years, driven by near-term fiscal challenges, will impact our national defense for decades to come. During the periods after protracted wars, the defense budget has historically declined and we have taken a "procurement holiday," which resulted in greater risk for the first battles of the next war. The impact takes into account the reality of defense spending – it rises and falls over time and is never constant. We will continue to refine our program investments under the following points:

- Smaller procurement objectives: As immediate operational and reset requirements decrease, the Army is refining the level of equipment we purchase annually as the Army cannot afford to equip and sustain the entire force with the most advanced equipment. The balance we struggle creating is to maintain operational readiness and fiscal responsibilities while also maintaining the industrial capacity to increase procurement when necessary.

- The Army will employ experiments and demonstration, such as the Network Integration Evaluations (NIE), to inform capabilities developed through Army research and development (R&D) processes. The NIE is a series of evaluations designed to put new technologies in the hands of Soldiers in a field environment early in the development process. The Army executes NIEs to evaluate emerging technologies from industry and government R&D, incorporating Soldier feedback into the acquisition process which results in more cost effective capability development.

- Align threshold requirements with mature/non-developmental technologies: Many capability gaps can be closed with equipment or technologies that already exist; commodity-like procurements will capitalize on industry practice to incrementally improve equipment as we unbundle our systems and requirements into components, sub-systems, and systems; this will also shorten acquisition timelines, enabling us to buy more often and divesting rather than sustaining some items.

- Cost-effectiveness is different than affordable: For the foreseeable future, every equipment decision has to be both affordable within the overall budget to include life cycle logistics costs, but also cost-effective in addressing the known capability gap that is being addressed; the opportunity cost of "over-spending" to close a specific gap is that we will not be able to afford closing other gaps; we will make cost-informed trades to manage risk.

- Setting requirements to be affordable: In the past, we spent large sums to develop programs that we later could not afford or the capability gap changed; we seek to minimize development times to preclude a forced "procurement holiday" while also assessing standing requirements that we have decided not to fund to determine if those requirements should be cancelled.

- Divest to reduce costs: To generate additional resources for modernization, we will accept risk by divesting older systems or niche capabilities to decrease sustainment costs; when planning platform replacements and upgrades, assess the economically sustainable life of the current platforms to determine cost and risk of continuing to sustain, upgrade or replace the platform.

- Invest for sustainability: When acquiring or upgrading capabilities, consider alternatives to reduce energy and water demands and develop operationally viable alternatives to reduce the tactical and operational risk to Soldiers.

SUMMARY

Our top priority remains ensuring our Soldiers are fully trained, equipped and ready to support current operations. Virtually all equipment coming out of Iraq and Afghanistan will require reset. Even after the drawdown from Afghanistan is complete, the Army will require funding for three years to reset our equipment from the harsh demands of war.

As we look to defense guidance and the future, the Army is a key Joint Force asset and the world's decisive land force. Soldiers and squads must be equipped, enabled, and prepared to operate in complex and uncertain battlefields supported by needed information and overmatch capabilities delivered to the right place, at the right time, to accomplish their mission. The Army can prevent conflict by maintaining credibility based on: dominant capabilities, readiness, environments shaped by sustained strong relationships with other

Armies, building their capacity, and facilitating strategic access. If necessary, the Army rapidly applies its combined arms capabilities in a "discriminately lethal" fashion to deter and defeat any adversary. In pursuing this equipment strategy, we must equip the Army for many missions, under many conditions, in varied geographies, against evolving threats, in an uncertain fiscal environment. Overall, our modernization efforts will prepare the Total Force for complex and uncertain battlefield by putting a squad with precise information and overmatch capability in the right place at the right time to accomplish their mission.

As current budget realities challenge steady funding for programs and limit our investment resources, we must make decisions on cost effective and affordable solutions with investments in key capabilities to provide the Force needed to meet combatant commanders' requirements and provide necessary alternatives for our Nation. We believe the President's Budget request for the Army does that.

Army Fiscal Year 2014 Budget Objectives and Priorities

ARMY FISCAL YEAR 2014
BUDGET OBJECTIVES AND PRIORITIES

The Soldier and Squad are the foundation of our Army. The American Soldier remains the most discriminately lethal force on the battlefield. Army equipment modernization builds from the Soldier out, equipping our squads for tactical overmatch in all situations, connected to an integrated network, and operating in vehicles that improve mobility and lethality while preserving survivability. Our plan provides our small units over time with a range of equipment to provide him with an advantage including individual and crew-served weapons, next generation optics and night vision devices, body armor and advanced individual protection equipment, providing lethality and force protection to the Soldier on the ground. For the Squad, tactical overmatch will be facilitated by a suite of small-unit systems including unmanned aerial vehicles, ground based robots, counter-IED devices, and the latest surveillance systems.

The Army Network and Mission Command connect Soldiers across the Joint Force linking them to the right information from a range of sensors and data sources at the right time to make the best possible decisions. It provides the squad connectivity with Joint assets, allowing access to Joint firepower systems in the most complex physical and human terrain.

Our combat and tactical wheeled vehicles and aviation improvements enable our forces with greater lethality, mobility and responsiveness. Overall, our modernization efforts will prepare the entire force for the complex and uncertain battlefield by putting a squad with precise information and overmatch capability in the right place at the right time to accomplish their mission.

The Army's FY 14 budget request supports the Defense strategy, provides a variety of capabilities to ensure the combatant commanders get what they need to shape their environment and reflects the equipment needed to deter and defeat current and future threats. Below are the priorities and specific objectives that guide FY 14 equipment modernization investments.

Priorities	Objectives
Enhance the Soldier for Broad Joint Mission Support	Empower and enable squads with improved lethality, protection and situational awareness
Enable Mission Command	Facilitate Command and Control and decision-making with networked real-time data and connectivity with the Joint force
Remain Prepared for Decisive Action	Increase lethality and mobility while optimizing survivability for vehicle fleets

PRIORITY PROGRAMS

The priority Army programs for FY 14 are:

The Network

- **Warfighter Information Network-Tactical (WIN-T)** $1.3B ($272M Research, Development, Test and Evaluation (RDTE)/$1.0B Other Procurement, Army (OPA) provides the broadband backbone communications necessary for the tactical Army. It extends an Internet Protocol (IP) based satellite and line-of-sight communications network through the tactical force supporting telephone, data and video. FY 12 began the fielding of the second increment of WIN-T providing an initial on-the-move capability as well as a robust line-of-sight transmission network and greater satellite throughput down to company level for maneuver brigades and division headquarters. FY 18 begins fielding the third increment of WIN-T, providing full on-the-move capabilities as well as exponential improvements in throughput on the line of sight transmission network and enabling an aerial layer to thicken the network.

- **Family of Networked Tactical Radios** $402.1M (OPA) is the Army's future deployable mobile communications family of radio systems providing advanced joint tactical end-to-end networking data and voice communications to dismounted troops and aircraft platforms. Formally known as the Joint Tactical Radio Systems (JTRS), these multi-band/multi-mode radio capabilities leverage IP based technologies and provide network routing, embedded information assurance and simultaneous exchange of voice, data and video.

- **Joint Battle Command-Platform (JBC-P)** $110.6M ($7.4M RDTE/$103.2M OPA) is the next generation of Force XXI Battle Command

Brigade and Below / Blue Force Tracking and is the foundation for achieving affordable information interoperability and superiority on current and future battlefields and is the principal command and control/situation awareness (C2/SA) system for the Army and Marine Corps at the brigade level and-below.

- **Distributed Common Ground System-Army (DCGS-A)** $295M ($28M RDTE/$267M OPA) provides integrated Intelligence, Surveillance, Reconnaissance (ISR) Processing, Exploitation and Dissemination (PED) of airborne and ground sensor platforms providing commanders, at all levels, access to the Defense Intelligence Information Enterprise and leverages the entire national, joint, tactical and coalition ISR community. Modernizes and procures components for the DCGS-A program, DCGS-A fixed sites and data centers setting conditions for the Army's ISR component of the Common Operating Environment (COE). DCGS-A hardware and software will be integrated into select ISR current force Programs of Record (POR) systems to network enable and provide enhanced PED capabilities.

- **Nett Warrior** $122.6M ($41M RDTE / $81.6M OPA). Squads are the foundation of the decisive force and Soldiers are the centerpiece of the Army's formation. Nett Warrior (NW) is a dismounted Soldier worn mission command system providing unprecedented C2/SA capabilities supporting the dismounted combat leader. The design incorporates operational unit mission needs and leverages operational lessons learned, while maintaining power requirements in austere environments.

Combat Vehicles

- **Ground Combat Vehicle (GCV)** $592M (RDTE) is the Army's replacement program for the Infantry Fighting Vehicle (IFV) in Armored Brigade Combat Teams (ABCTs) and is the centerpiece of the Army's overall Combat Vehicle Modernization Strategy. The GCV accommodates a nine-man infantry squad, balances mobility and survivability, and provides improved lethality on the battlefield. Key GCV attributes include, required network integration, modular armor allowing commander adjustments based on operational threats as well as a design which allows incorporation of future size, weight, power, and cooling technologies (SWAP-C). The Army expects to award Engineering and Manufacturing Development (EMD) contracts in FY 14.

- **Armored Multi-Purpose Vehicle (AMPV)** $116M (RDTE) replaces the M113 family of vehicles and provides required protection, mobility and networking for the Army's critical enablers including mission command, mortars, medical evacuation and medical treatment as well as general purpose vehicles. Following the February 2012 Materiel Development Decision, an Analysis of Alternatives has been completed. The Army expects to award an Engineering and Manufacturing Development contract following Milestone B scheduled in third quarter FY 14.

- **Paladin Integrated Management (PIM)** $340.8M ($80.6M RDTE/$260.2M Weapons and Tracked Combat Vehicles (WTCV) is an important part of the Army's Ground Combat Vehicle Modernization Strategy and provides readily available, low risk upgrades enhancing the responsiveness, force protection, survivability and mobility of the self-propelled howitzer fleet. The PIM replaces the current M109A6 Paladin and M992A2 Field Artillery Ammunition Supply Vehicle with a more robust platform incorporating Bradley common drive train and suspension components in a newly designed hull. The program completed the

initial Developmental Testing phase and was designated as an Acquisition Category I Major Defense Acquisition Program in FY 11.

Light Tactical Vehicles

- **Joint Light Tactical Vehicle (JLTV)** $84.2M (RDTE) is the centerpiece of the Army's Tactical Wheeled Vehicle modernization strategy replacing approximately one third of the light wheeled vehicle fleet by 2041. The JLTV family of vehicles is being designed to provide the necessary leap in protection, performance, and payload to fill the capability gap remaining between the High Mobility Multipurpose Wheeled Vehicle (HMMWV) and the Mine Resistant Ambush Protected (MRAP) family of vehicles. This multi-mission vehicle will provide protected, sustained and networked mobility for personnel and payloads across the full range of military operations whether traditional or irregular. The Army anticipates a down select to one specific manufacture prior to Milestone (MS) C decision in 3rd Quarter FY 15 to determine the manufacturer to produce the first line of JLTVs.

Aviation

- **Kiowa Warrior (KW)** $257.8M ($69.8M RDTE/$184.0M Aviation Procurement, Army (ACFT)/$4M Operations & Maintenance, Army (OMA)). The Army recognizes a continuing requirement for a light, armed helicopter for manned armed aerial reconnaissance, surveillance and light attack operations missions. In addition to OH-58D Wartime Replacement Aircraft, this funding modernizes the Kiowa Warrior to the OH-58F model by providing enhanced cockpit and sensor capabilities through the Cockpit and Sensor Upgrade Program (CASUP).

Equipment Portfolio Overviews

SOLDIER AND SQUAD
SECTION 1— OVERVIEW

The squad is the foundation of the decisive force and the cornerstone of all units. Ensuring our squads have overmatch in the future, this portfolio focuses on equipping for squad success. Squad equipment and weapons include: small arms, crew-served weapons, shoulder-fired and vehicle-mounted missiles, mortars, Soldier sensors and lasers, night vision devices, body armor, Soldier clothing, individual equipment, parachutes, and limited tactical communications equipment (see figure 1). Collectively, these systems enable lethality, protection, situational awareness and mobility for the individual Soldier and squad.

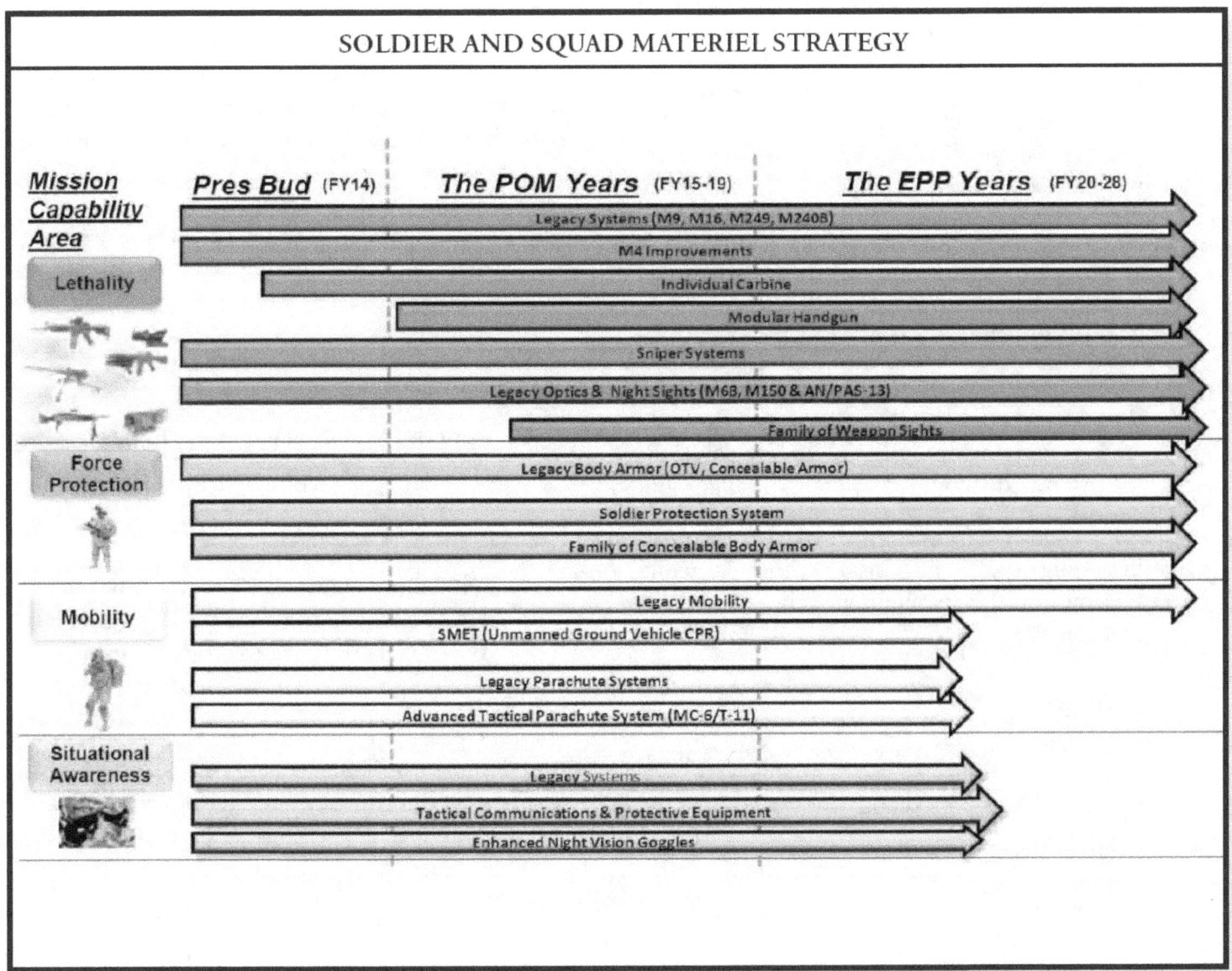

FIGURE 1. Soldier and Squad Portfolio (see Acronym Glossary)

To meet the readiness and the modernization objectives of the Army Campaign Plan the Soldier and Squad portfolio focus for FY 14 is:

- Supporting the Engineering and Manufacturing Development phase of the XM-25, Counter Defilade Target Engagement (CDTE) system is the next step in employing this revolutionary Soldier-level, precision weapon system.

- Continuing the fielding of Enhanced Night Vision Devices to deploying Special Operation Forces and Brigade Combat Teams.

- Executing small arms procurement, as informed by the results of a full and open carbine competition, while simultaneously improving the current carbine capability for deployed forces.

- Continuing replacement of the conventional force parachute inventory with the Advanced Tactical Parachute System.

- Continuing Soldier load reduction efforts through research and development in body armor, weapons and selected energy solutions to extend dismounted Soldiers' range and endurance.

- Providing the Fire Resistant Environmental Ensemble to aircrews improving their protection and comfort.

- Continue fielding of Operation Enduring Freedom Camouflage Pattern Fire Resistant Army Combat Uniforms and organizational and individual equipment to forces deploying to Afghanistan which will help inform future Army uniform camouflage strategy.

Section II — Key Soldier and Squad Portfolio Accomplishments (FY 12/13):

- Reduced Soldier load in Afghanistan by replacing 501 M240B Medium Machine Guns with Lightweight Medium Machine Guns (10 pounds) and 44,000 Outer Tactical Vests with plate carriers (3.2 pounds). In addition, reduced the weight of the 81mm Mortar by 20 pounds and the 60mm Mortar by 8.8 pounds.

- Provided the American Soldier with the best possible carbine by procuring improved M4A1s (rather than M4 Carbines) and converting existing M4 Carbines into improved M4A1s. Capability improvements include a heavier barrel for greater barrel life, fully automatic trigger and selector switch, ambidextrous controls, improved sustained rate of fire, a consistent trigger pull and improved ergonomics and handling characteristics.

- Continued procuring the following small arms weapon initiatives with:

  >> 12,000 M4A1 Carbines from new production to support the industrial base, while procuring the parts to convert even more M4s to M4A1s.

  >> 5,402 kits to convert .50 cal Machine guns to Quick-Change Barrel (QCB) Variants to eliminate the need to set Head Space & Timing.

- Limited procurement and increased research and development of Soldier night vision equipment for current and future contingencies enhancing Soldier lethality and situational awareness across the full range of missions:

  >> 2,195 Sniper Night Sights for Special Operations Forces (SOF), Brigade

Combat Teams (BCTs) and Battlefield Surveillance Brigades.

>> 27,765 Thermal Weapon Sights for deploying BCTs, Combat Support (CS) and SOF units.

>> 1,301 Laser Target Locators for BCTs.

>> 372 Small Tactical Optical Rifle-Mounted (STORM) (micro laser range finders) for dismounted infantry and scouts in BCTs.

>> 1,059 Enhanced Night Vision Goggles for deploying BCTs and SOF units.

Section III — Key FY 14 Soldier and Squad Portfolio Investments:

The FY 14 Soldier investments total $1.1B ($115M RDTE/$295M WTCV/$377M OPA/$200M Missile Procurement, Army (MSLS)/$109M OMA) and include small arms (individual and crew-served weapons), night vision, Soldier sensors, body armor, individual networked command and control (C2), Soldier clothing and individual equipment, and parachutes. Specific investments in this portfolio include:

- $167M (OPA) procures Enhanced Night Vision Goggles for deploying SOF and 6,147 systems per deploying BCT.

- $31.6M (WTCV) continues small arms investment consisting of M4A1 procurement which supports the industrial base; converting M4s to M4A1s; and procuring carbine accessories (Close Combat Optics, M4 Rails, Close Quarters Battle Kits, Cleaning Kits and Magazines). The M4A1 provides Soldiers with close quarters capability at extended ranges with accurate lethal fire.

- Full spectrum dominance Soldier sensors and lasers for deploying BCTs and SOF:

>> $30.9M (OPA) procures 658 Laser Target Locators.

>> $22.3M (OPA) procures 1,491 STORM (micro laser range finders).

- $46M (OPA) fields new parachutes and accessories for three BCTs.

- $24.0M (WTCV) for 5,061 M320A1 40MM Grenade Launchers.

- $56.6M (WTCV) for 242 Common Remotely Operated Weapon Station (CROWS).

- $49.6M (WTCV) for 29,987 Individual Carbines.

- $33.7M (WTCV) for 3,238 QCB Kits to convert M2 (.50 Cal) Machine Guns to M2A1s.

- Begin upgrading all Improved Target Acquisition System (ITAS) systems with Network Lethality and Image Enhancement to increase overall Tube-Launched, Optically-Tracked, Wire-Guided (TOW) lethality.

Mission Command
Section 1 — Overview

LandWarNet (LWN) 2020 And Beyond is the Army's End-to-End Network that simultaneously supports all Army Mission Areas. The Mission Command portfolio is the Operational segment of this network which supports Service, Joint, Coalition, and Interagency operations (see figure 2). This portfolio consists of four distinct capability areas: Transport, Applications, Enablers and Integration. Warfighter Information Network – Tactical (WIN-T) and the Family of Networked Tactical Radios are the primary Transport programs; Tactical Battle Command (TBC), Joint Battle Command – Platform (JBC-P) and Global Combat Support System – Army (GCSS-A) are the key Application programs; Communication Security (COMSEC) with Key Management Infrastructure and Power Generation are the key Network Enabler programs; and

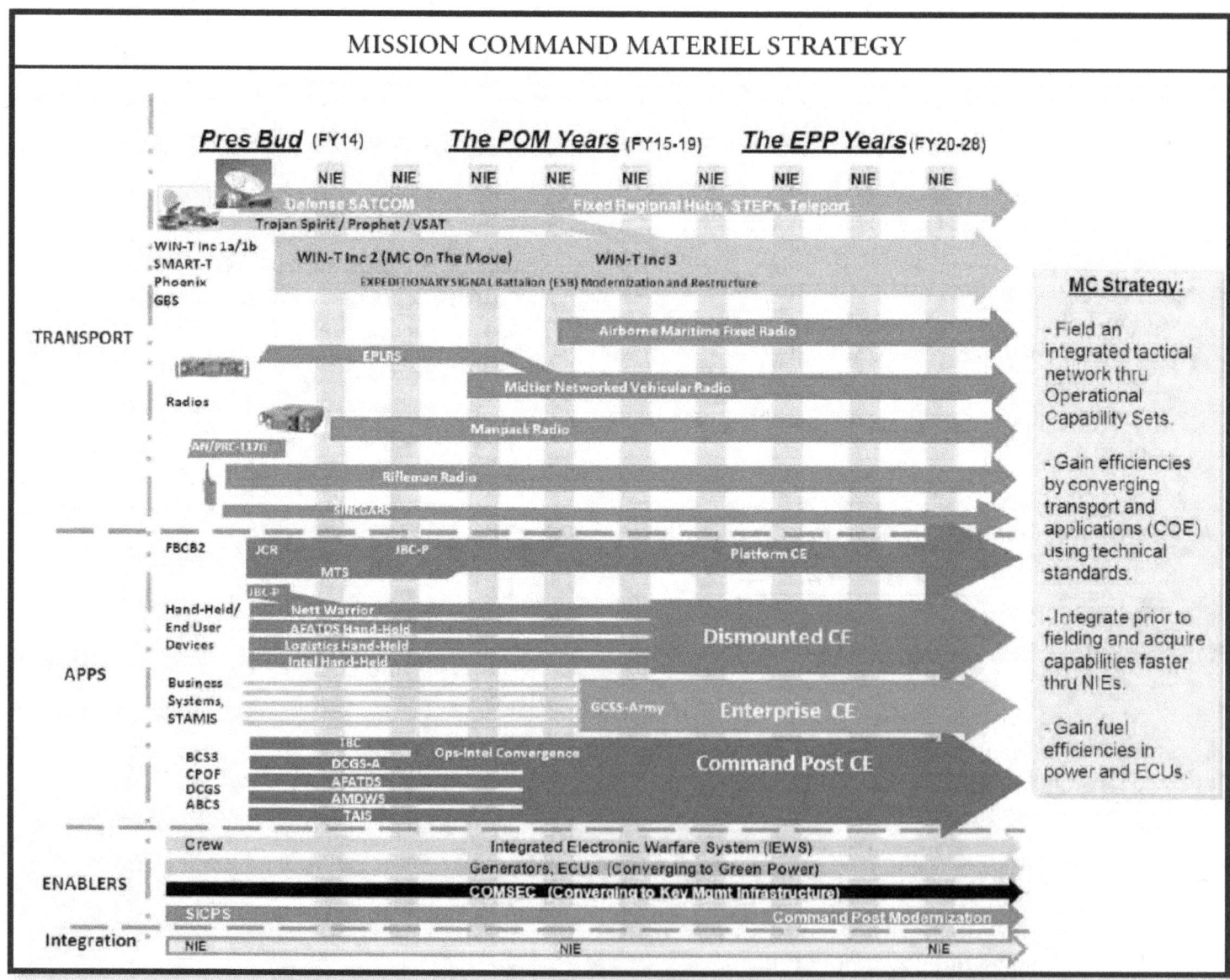

FIGURE 2. Mission Command Portfolio (see Acronym Glossary)

NIE is the principal integration program. The Army integrates these elements into a coherent, intuitive network of sensors, Soldiers, platforms, and command posts linked by a robust transport network with an enabling suite of C2 applications, plus the necessary Network Operations (NetOps) tools providing our Soldiers greater access to varied and defendable network capabilities.

The network supports both the operating and generating force, shares information across levels of classification and enables rapid application development and deployment. The network is the combat multiplier for a flexible Army and every Soldier has enabled access.

Section II — Key Mission Command Portfolio Accomplishments (FY 12/13):

- Fielding of Capability Set 13 (CS13) to five Brigade Combat Teams and two Division headquarters. CS13 provides the first fully integrated Networking on-the-move capability through networking radios, satellite systems, software applications, and smartphone like devices developed as a result of Soldier-driven evaluations during the NIE process.

- Completed the fielding of WIN-T Increment (Inc) 1 and Inc 1a initial capabilities to 210 units. In an effort that began in FY 12, all Inc 1 and 1a units will be upgraded to Inc 1b providing Enhanced Networking at the Halt capabilities by introducing the Net Centric Waveform modem and the "colorless core" for interoperability.

- Conducted the Initial Operational Test and Evaluation (IOTE) for WIN-T Inc 2 providing an initial on-the-move capability and extending the network to the company level. Fielded initial Inc 2 to support CS13 Units.

- Completed the reshaping of the former JTRS programs. Conducted the IOTE for the Handheld, Manpack, and Small Form Fit (HMS) ManPack (MP) and Rifleman Radio (RR) resulting in direction to procure and field the initial Rifleman Radio capabilities and direction to procure the initial HMS MP capability. Fielded initial RR and HMS MP capabilities to support CS13 units.

- Began the fielding of an Advanced Medium Mobile Power Source (AMMPS), designed to integrate with distributed renewable power generation, power storage and power management solutions, in support of Security Forces Assistance Advisory Teams (SFAATs), Village Stability Platforms (VSPs) and austere combat outposts. AMMPS generators replace the Tactical Quiet Generators, are Environmental Protection Agency (EPA) compliant and provide a 21 percent improvement fleet-wide in fuel efficiency. Further fuel reductions are being obtained at selected forward operating bases where we have integrated mini-grids with AMMPS.

- Completed development of Command Post of the Future (CPOF) 7.0, culminating a four year effort to engineer the system to support continuous operations in all network environments. With this delivery in FY 12, CPOF gives the Soldier the ability to operate in disconnected, intermittent, and latent network environments and automatically re-synchronizing offline data changes when the network becomes available.

- Began development of Mission Command collapse, which provides a significantly enhanced Common Operating Picture (COP) and collaboration experience through an automated interface on the Mission Command workstation for intelligence, fires, logistics management and airspace management. This frees the Soldier by eliminating countless hours and effort of having to swivel chair or manually input specific war fighting function data into the COP.

- Implemented the Command Post Computing Environment (CP CE) under the Common Operating Environment (COE), which provides a significantly enhanced COP and collaboration through an interface on a consolidated Mission Command workstation for intelligence, fires, logistics management and airspace management tools and applications in a more intuitive and cost effective manner. Formalized the COE effort by assigning responsibility for leading the various Computing Environments, including Command Posts, Mounted, and Mobile/ Hand Held.

- Implemented the series of NIE events to ensure integrated network capabilities are delivered to units rather than separate systems which require integration. NIE also provides the Army with a mechanism to rapidly and cost-effectively evaluate and assess commercial upgrades and capabilities for Army use.

Section III — Key FY 14 Mission Command Investments:

FY 14 Mission Command investments total $3.6B ($844M RDTE/$2.4B OPA / $369M OMA) and include communications transport, applications and network services capabilities. Specific investments in this portfolio include:

- $293M (OPA) procures WIN-T Increment 1b upgrading 77 Brigades.

- $712M (OPA) procures WIN-T Increment 2 equipping four BCTs and two Divisions and spares.

- $272M (RDTE) continues the development of WIN-T Increment 3 to include an integrated

NetOps, Aerial Layer and the convergence of the intelligence network into the WIN-T network.

- $402.1M (OPA) procures Mid-Tier Networking Vehicular Radio (MNVR) systems, HMS ManPack radios and Rifleman Radios for BCTs.

- $103.2M (OPA) procures Joint Battle Command-Platform (JBC-P) for BCTs and BDEs.

- $7.4M (RDTE) supports implementation of Mounted Computing Environment (MCE) as part of COE.

- $36.5M (RDTE) resources development efforts for Command Post COE server infrastructure/ common software, interoperability, COE mission command application modifications, operations/intelligence convergence and the rich web client/command web capability.

- $101.4M (OPA) provides continued procurement of AMMPS.

- $194M (RDTE) and $20M (OPA) resources two NIEs per fiscal year and enables the procurement of limited new technology as a result of the new approach to agile acquisition in the NIE process.

- $41.2M (RDTE) and $83.9M (OPA), achieves the GCSS-A Full Deployment Decision (FDD), begins training and fielding of Wave 1 to all Supply Support Activities Army wide, continues development of Wave 2 consisting of unit supply, ground maintenance and property book.

INTELLIGENCE

SECTION 1— OVERVIEW

The Intelligence Portfolio incorporates key components of intelligence collection, exploitation, and analysis across four primary layers: Foundational, Terrestrial, Aerial and Space. The goal of the portfolio is to fully integration the core intelligence capabilities, including Signals Intelligence (SIGINT) collection, Counterintelligence (CI)/Human Intelligence (HUMINT) interrogation and source operations, and Geospatial Intelligence (GEOINT), including Full Motion Video (FMV). The portfolio also includes secure intelligence communications architecture, synchronized and integrated with the Army's network initiatives. This architecture supports all aspects of exploitation, analysis, and dissemination to meet the readiness and modernization objectives of the Army Campaign Plan.

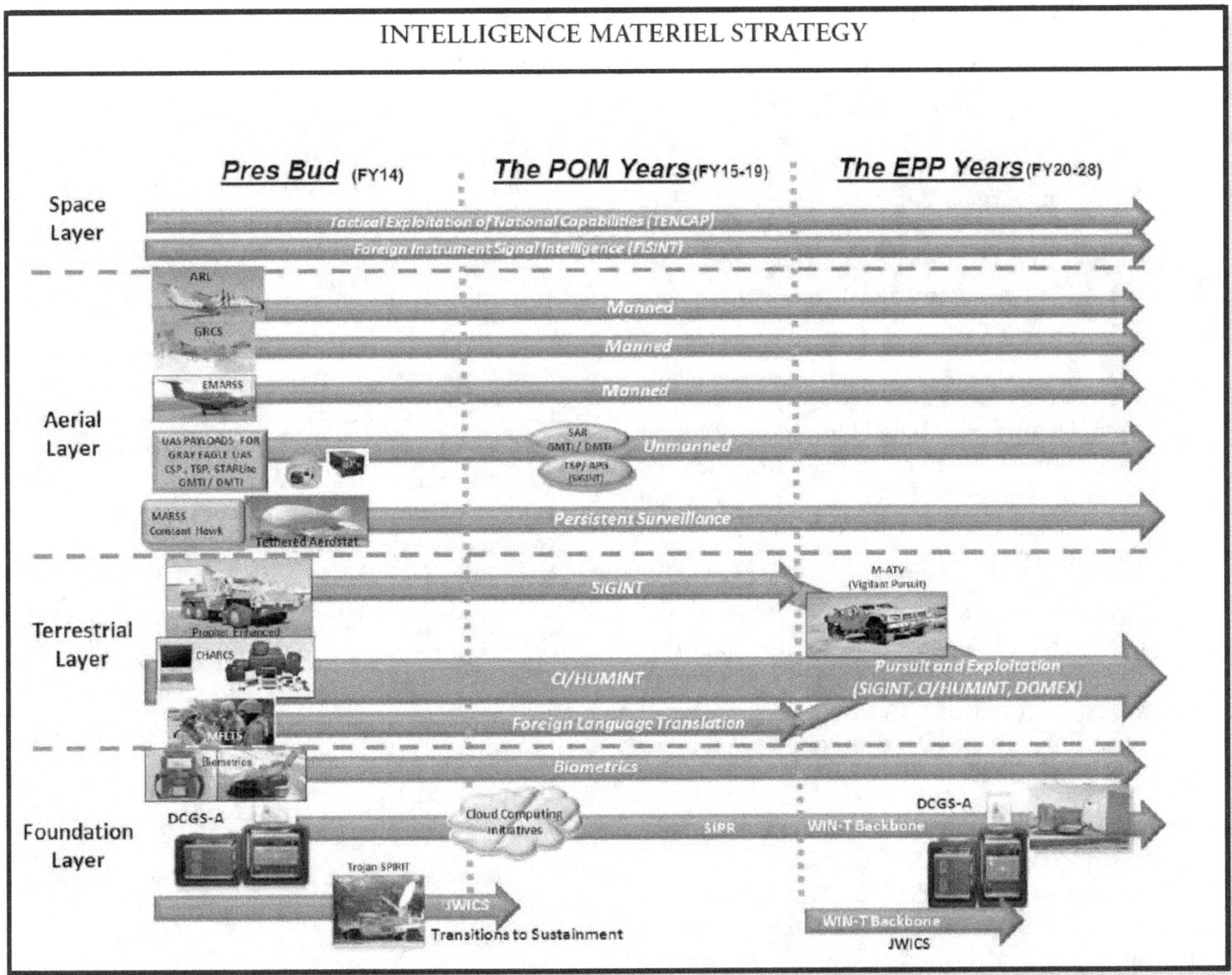

FIGURE 3. Intelligence Portfolio (see Acronym Glossary)

As depicted in figure 3 (pg. 31), the Intelligence portfolio provides essential modernization to keep pace with the evolving threat and rapid technological advancements.

- Fully funds the Distributed Common Ground System – Army (DCGS-A)

- Fully funds the Enhanced Medium Altitude Reconnaissance and Surveillance System (EMARSS)

- Fully funds the Prophet Ground SIGINT capability

Section II – Key Intelligence
Portfolio Accomplishments (FY 12/13):

- Continued the transition of DCGS-A Operation Enduring Freedom (OEF) capabilities to "cloud computing" architecture, with user gateways from Company Intelligence Support Team (CoIST) to the International Security Assistance Force Headquarters.

  >> Began training the cloud software baseline.

- Completed a formal Initial Operational Test and Evaluation (IOT&E) of DCGS-A in FY 12. The Defense Acquisition Executive published a Full Deployment Decision (FDD) Memorandum in December 2012.

- Achieved EMARSS Milestone (MS) B and entered the EMD phase with contract award for four to six EMD EMARSS aircraft to the Boeing Corporation. Began development and initial testing of these EMD aircraft in preparation for MS C in FY 14.

- Procured and integrated Enhanced Situational Awareness (ESA) and High Band Communications Intelligence (COMINT) (HBC) on the remaining seven RC-12X GUARDRAIL Common Sensor (GRCS) systems for fielding in FY 12. Retrofits the

first seven modernized GRCS with improvements to COMINT ESA, Communications High Accuracy Location System, and HBC in FY 13.

- Continued Airborne Reconnaissance – Low (ARL) upgrades of system payloads with improvements to interface software and radar in FY 12 remaining a relevant ISR collection asset against a dynamic range of targets. of targets. Provided interoperable data links and workstation architecture software in FY 13 to improve workstation performance.

- Equipped and fielded the Gray Eagle Unmanned Aircraft System (UAS) in FY 12 and FY 13 with the Common Sensor Payload (CSP), which includes Full Motion Video (Electro-Optical/Infrared/Laser Designator). Also equipped the Gray Eagle UAS with the Small Tactical Radar Lightweight (STARLite) sensor, a Synthetic Aperture Radar (SAR) that provides imagery through weather and detects moving target indicators. RDTE efforts initiated engineering development of High Definition (HD) video improvements for CSP, enhancements to STARLite range, and resolution and initiation of EMD of the Tactical SIGINT Payload (TSP). TSP testing will be delayed by six months, delaying the completion of TSP EMD Block 1 Increment 1 from July 2013 to July 2014.

- Fielded Prophet Enhanced Ground SIGINT, a more modular and vehicle-agnostic version of Prophet Signals Intelligence collection capability, to BCTs and Battlefield Surveillance Brigades (BfSBs) operating in combat theaters.

  >> Fielded 12 of the Prophet Enhanced sensors to next deployers as Theater Provided Equipment (TPE) in FY 12. Provided RDTE for software and hardware upgrades to the Prophet Enhanced sensors in order to maintain operational relevance.

>> Fielded five Prophet Enhanced sensors to next deployers as TPE in FY 13. Provided RDTE for continued software and hardware upgrades to the Prophet Enhanced sensors.

SECTION III –KEY FY 14 INTELLIGENCE PORTFOLIO INVESTMENTS:

The FY 14 Intelligence portfolio investments total $766M ($154M RDTE / $349M OPA / $263M ACFT) and include the key components of ISR collection, exploitation, and analysis. Specific investments in this portfolio include:

- $295M ($267M OPA/$28M RDTE) funds DCGS-A development and procurement to modernize and procure components for the DCGS-A Program, DCGS-A fixed sites, and Data Centers, setting conditions for the Army's ISR component of the COE. DCGS-A hardware and software will be integrated into select ISR current force platforms to network enable and provide enhanced ISR PED capabilities.

  >> Provides development and testing of DCGS-A multi-intelligence capable software baselines as well as the continued development and testing of the Command Post Computing Environment as it fits into the Army's overarching COE construct.

  >> Procures 2,303 DCGS-A Portable Multi-Function Workstations, 88 Fixed – Multi Functional Workstations, 94 GEOINT Workstations, three DCGS-A ISR Process Center V1s, 15 DCGS-A ISR Process Center V2s, one Operational ISR Ground Station, one DCGS-A Global Unified Data Environment Node, and 18 Cross Domain Systems and 194 Intelligence Fusion Servers. These systems will support one corps, three divisions, 12 BCTs, three special operations units,

three maneuver enhancement brigades, three combat aviation brigades, three fires brigades, Army Materiel Command (AMC) Intelligence Directorate, and other combat support (CS) and combat service support (CSS) units entering the Army Force Generation (ARFORGEN) available pool.

- $152.5M ($142.1M ACFT; $10.4M RDTE) funds development and procurement for EMARSS to provide a real-time, networked multi-sensor intelligence collection capability throughout the joint battlespace, with focus on support to BCT operations.

  >> Completes EMD phase, including all test and evaluation activities.

  >> Procures four Low Rate Initial Production (LRIP) systems.

- $10.3M (ACFT) completes SIGINT Payload modernization and begins FMV integration for Guardrail Common Sensor.

- $12.5M (ACFT) supports procurement of a mission equipment package to install sensors that support a plug-and-play mounting system to allow rapid integration of sensors for ARL.

  >> Procures workstation architecture for one system, workstation, servers, monitors, and communications equipment.

- $128.1M ($97.8M ACFT/$30.3M RDTE) for UAS ISR Payloads, providing the Gray Eagle platform with day and night capability to collect and display FMV continuous imagery, wide-area all-weather search capability, persistent stare, Ground Moving Target Indicator (GMTI), and SAR capabilities.

  >> Provides development of UAS payloads and procurement of eight CSP Electro-Optical/

Infrared/Laser Designator (EO/IR/LD) equipped with HD sensors, 23 CSP HD Retrofits, and eight STARLite SAR/GMTI sensors and 16 TSP sensors for integration and fielding support to the ARFORGEN schedule. RDTE facilitates continued improvements to CSP and STARLite and baseline development of TSP.

- $65.3M ($59.2M OPA/$6.1M RDTE) for Prophet Ground SIGINT.

  >> Procures nine Prophet Enhanced sensors mounted on Panther Medium Mine Protected Vehicles for training and fielding to BCTs and BfSBs operating in combat theaters.

>> Funding will also procure three next-generation antennas and hardware/software improvements to keep pace with rapidly changing threat technology, tactics, techniques, and procedures.

>> Funds RDTE product upgrades for next-generation signals and multi-path/co-site mitigation for pre-planned product improvement requirements for Prophet Enhanced sensors.

Ground Movement and Maneuver

Section 1— Overview

The Ground Movement and Maneuver Portfolio's goal is to develop and field an integrated combined team, linked by the network, and capable of dominating across the range of missions today and into the future. Key to this effort is our Combat Vehicle Modernization Strategy which transforms the capability of the Brigade Combat Team by acquiring the Ground Combat Vehicle (GCV) and replacing the M113 Family of Vehicles with an Armored-Multi Purpose Vehicle AMPV). The strategy also improves the Abrams tank; the Bradley Cavalry, Fire Support, and Engineer Vehicles; and the Stryker by increasing protection, ensuring required mobility, and allowing integration of the network.

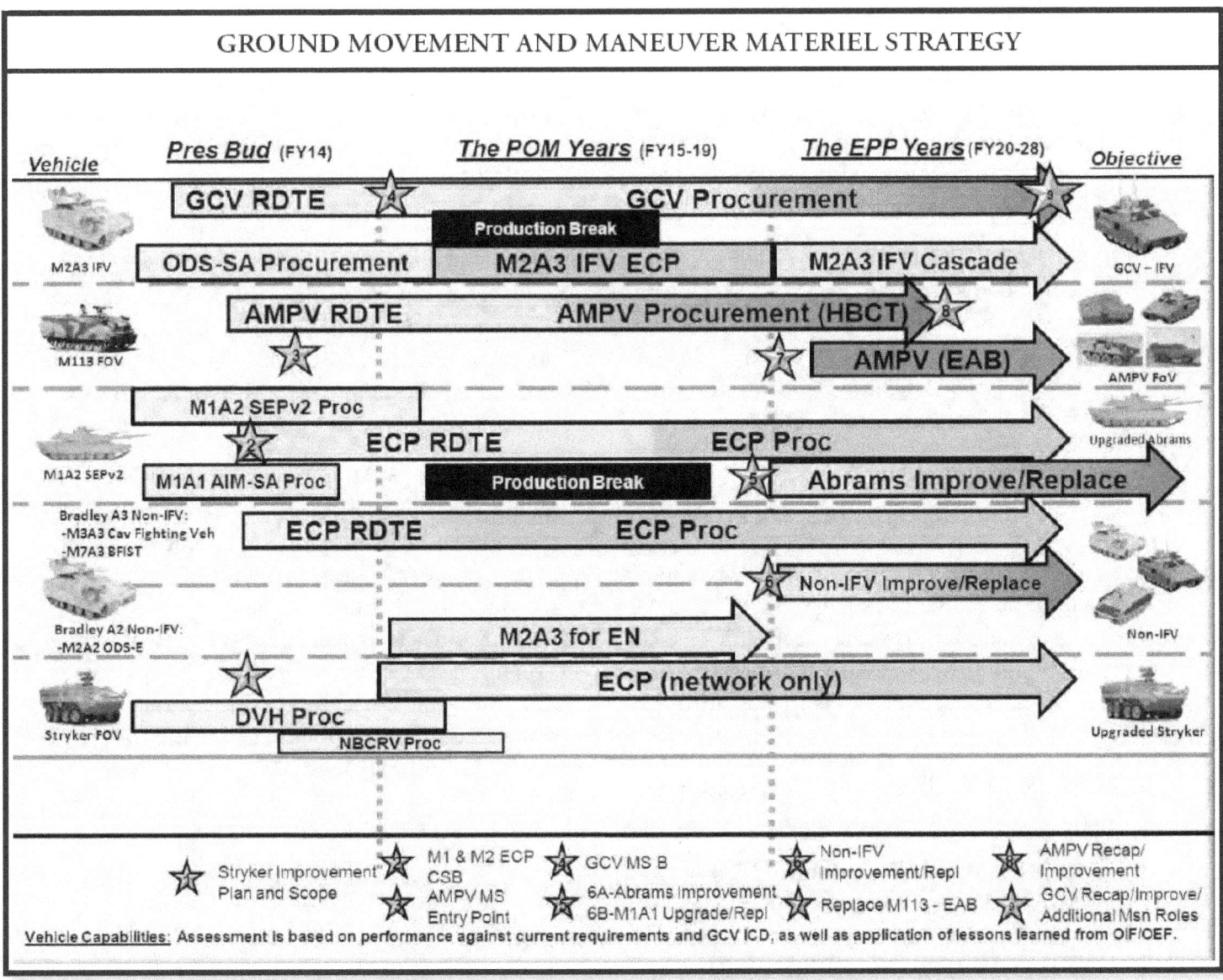

FIGURE 4. Ground Movement and Maneuver Portfolio (see Acronym Glossary)

Section II – Key Ground Movement and Maneuver Portfolio Accomplishments (FY 12/13)

- Modernizes 1st Infantry Division (Fort Riley) and the 116th ABCT (Idaho Army National Guard) with the most modern versions of the Abrams tank (M1A2 System Enhancement Program (SEP) v2) and the Bradley Fighting Vehicle (M2A3). The 155th ABCT (Mississippi Army National Guard) will also field the M1A2 SEP v2 to complement the M2A3 Bradley Fighting Vehicles that were fielded in 2012.

- Continue our focus on achieving standardization of two variants of our dominant combat maneuver platforms (M1 Abrams Tank and M2 Bradley Fighting Vehicle (BFV)) combined with expansion of the versatile and lethal Stryker Combat Vehicle.

  >> Upgraded kits made the M2A3 Operation Desert Storm (ODS) and M3A2 ODS Bradleys compatible with the M1A1 SA Abrams, providing greater lethality, survivability, and sustainability.

Section III –Key FY 14 Ground Movement and Maneuver Portfolio Investments:

The FY 14 Ground Movement and Maneuver investments total $1.8B ($870M WTCV/ $943M RDTE) and include the Army's combat vehicles such as Abrams, Bradley, Stryker, and the development of the GCV. Specific investments in this portfolio include:

- $592M (RDTE) develops GCV technologies which continue through 3rd quarter FY 14.

- $374M ($168M RDTE / $206M OPA) begins M109A6 PIM procurement by purchasing the Paladin Digital Fire Control System-Replacement. RDTE funds the development and integration of common components into prototype vehicles.

- $116M (RDTE) funds AMPV Pre-Milestone B development activities with a Milestone B Defense Acquisition Board (DAB) planned for 3rd quarter, FY 14.

- $49.9M (RDTE) funds Stryker Engineering Change Proposal (ECP) that addresses future network integration, mobility, and SWaP-C. The Stryker ECP provides growth in electrical, mechanical, and engine power.

- $394M (WTCV) funds a third Double-V-Hull (DVH) brigade through the Stryker Exchange Program in FY 14-16 and fielding of Nuclear Biological Chemical Reconnaissance Vehicles (NBCRV).

- $279M ($178M WTCV/$101M RDTE) completes the fielding of M1A2 SEP v2 Abrams and achieves Modular Two Variant Fleet Configuration which is 1,593 M1A2 SEP v2s and 791 M1A1 AIM SA. RDTE funds the technology development phase for Abrams ECP improvements.

- $234M ($158M WTCV/$76M RDTE) completes the fielding of Bradley ODS-Situational Awareness (SA) vehicles to the Army National Guard (ARNG) and continues production of ECP1 capability that restores lost ground clearance due to increased combat weight. RDTE focuses on ECP improvements for the Bradley Cavalry, Fire Support, and Engineer Vehicles focused on mobility and SWaP-C improvements.

Aviation

Section 1— Overview

The Aviation portfolio consists of core aviation programs, including utility and cargo, fixed wing mission profiles, reconnaissance/attack, Intelligence, Surveillance and Reconnaissance (ISR), and Unmanned Aircraft Systems (UAS) which meet the readiness and modernization objectives of the Army Campaign Plan.

As depicted within figures five through seven, key objectives and decision points in the Aviation portfolio are:

- Fully fund the Kiowa Warrior OH-58F program.

- Fully fund the Apache AH-64E (Apache Block III) program.

- Fully fund Gray Eagle UAS production.

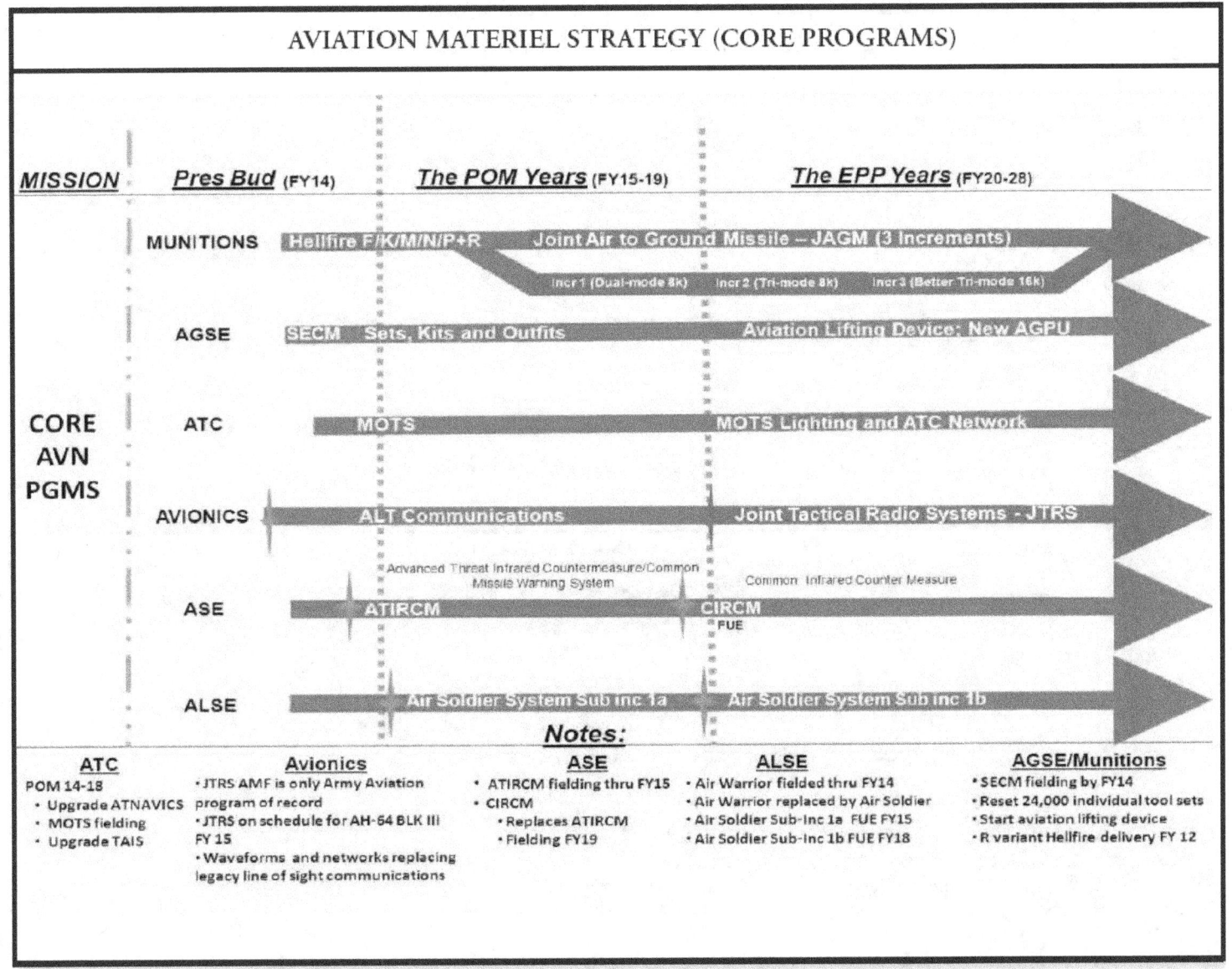

FIGURE 5. Aviation Portfolio (Core Programs) (see Acronym Glossary)

- Fully fund UH-60 production, meeting 4th ID Combat Aviation Brigade (CAB) growth and the increased aircraft requirement for Special Operations.

- Complete procurement of the Lakota Light Utility Helicopter program at 315 aircraft, 31 short of the Army Acquisition Objective.

- Fully fund the 13th CAB and Special Operations CH-47 aircraft requirements.

SECTION II—KEY AVIATION ACCOMPLISHMENTS (FY 12/13):

- Continued induction of Apache AH-64D Block I helicopters for remanufacture to AH-64E (Apache Block III).

- Continued equipping of the Advanced Threat Infrared Countermeasures (ATIRCM) on the CH-47D/F helicopters.

- Continued upgrading the Raven UAS to Digital

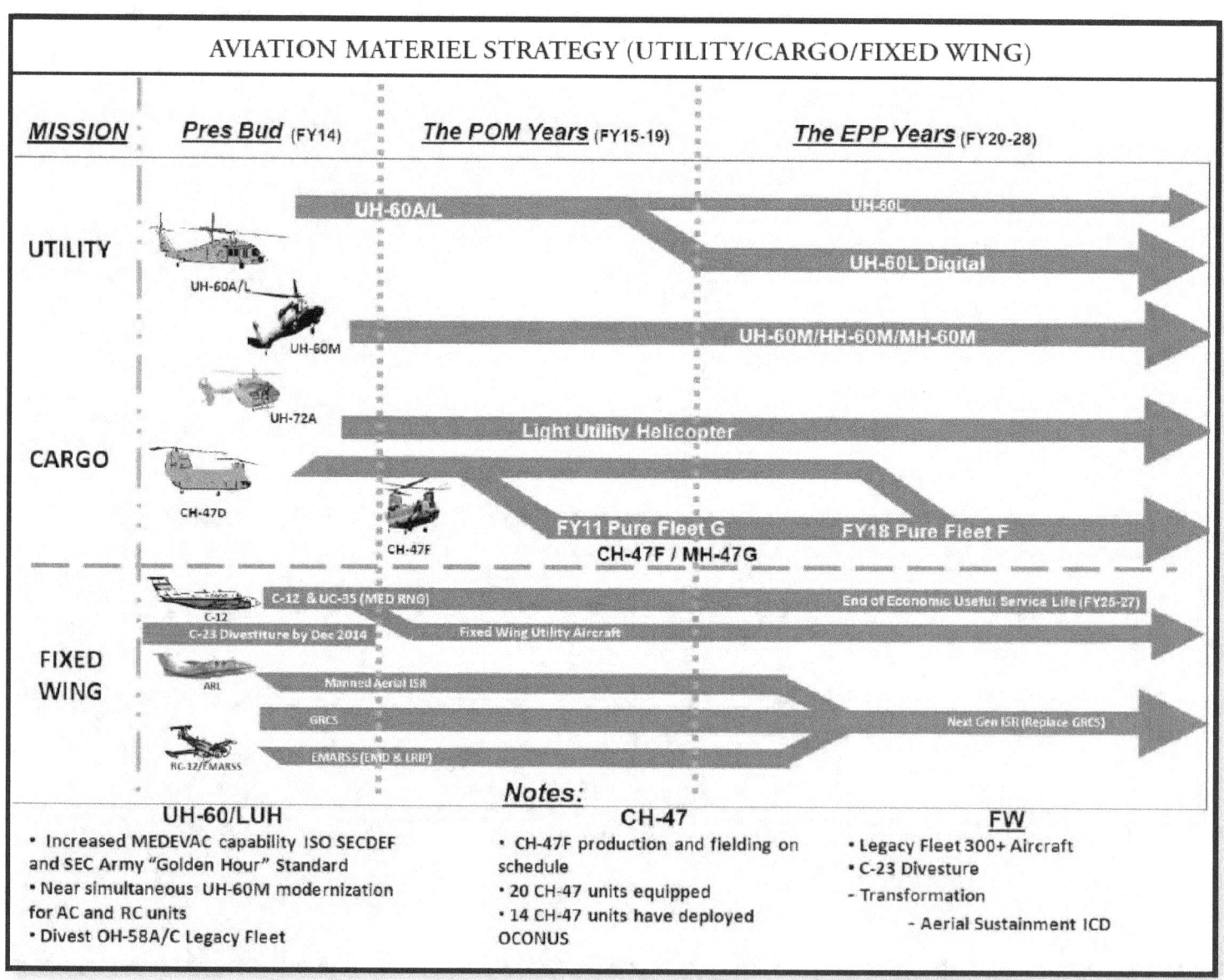

FIGURE 6. Aviation Portfolio (Utility/Cargo/Fixed Wing) (see Acronym Glossary)

Data Link (DDL) with 84 DDL systems fielded in FY 12, 377 new systems procured, and 332 analog systems converted to DDL. DDL increases the amount of channels Raven aircraft use within a single geographic area, providing the supported unit more FMV coverage across the area of operations.

- Fielded the 1-135th Attack Reconnaissance Battalion (ARB) (Missouri ARNG) with AH-64D Apache Block II helicopters; also continued

fielding the 1-183rd (ARB) (Idaho ARNG) and 1-149th ARB (Texas/Mississippi ARNG) with AH-64D Apache Block II helicopters.

- In FY 12, procured and fielded components of the Air Warrior System (to include the new Operation Enduring Freedom Camouflage Pattern flight uniform) to deploying CAB's aircrew members. In FY 13 complete procurement of the Air Warrior System, with fielding completed to the Army in FY 14.

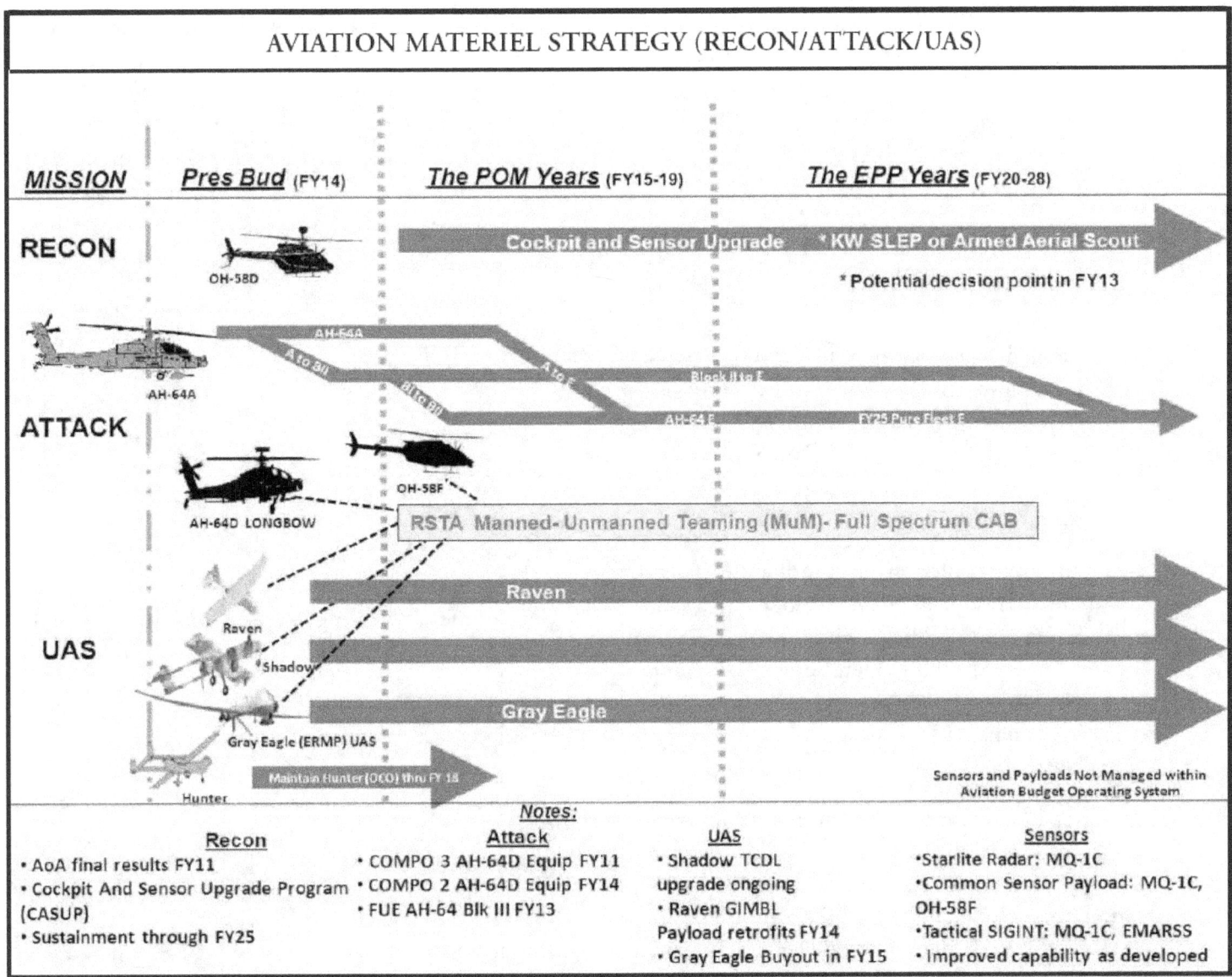

FIGURE 7. *Aviation Portfolio (RECON/ATTACK/UAS) (see Acronym Glossary)*

- Fielded Medical Evacuation (MEDEVAC) helicopters (HH-60M) to four General Support Aviation Battalions, supporting Army and Department of Defense leadership emphasis on increased MEDEVAC Capability.

- Procured 19 MQ-1C Gray Eagle Unmanned Aircraft and the associated ground support equipment ($518.1M). Gray Eagle missions include Reconnaissance, Surveillance, Target Acquisition, Armed Reconnaissance, Signals Intelligence, Communications Relay, and Battle Damage Assessment.

  >> Fielded two Gray Eagle Quick Reaction Capability platoons equipped with four aircraft each, both of which were deployed in support of OEF.

  >> Completed fielding the first MQ-1C Gray Eagle Company to the 1st Cavalry Division CAB and the unit which deployed in FY 12.

  >> Fielded the second MQ-1C Gray Eagle Company to the 1st Infantry Division CAB in the 3rd quarter of FY 12. The unit conducted Initial Operational Test and Evaluation in August 2012 and subsequently deployed.

  >> Upon completion of the fielding plan, the Army will have fielded 13 Gray Eagle Companies with two assigned to the Special Operations Command, one to each active component division headquarters (ten total), and one to the National Training Center.

- Procured Shadow modifications including seven Tactical Common Data Link (TCDL) Retrofit Kits, seven launchers, nine Universal Mission Simulators, 80 New Mission Computers, and 14 SIGINT payloads. New Equipment Training for TCDL Retrofits continues through FY 14.

- Focused rotary wing aircraft modernization on the UH-60 (Black Hawk), CH-47 (Chinook), and AH-64 (Apache) helicopters:

  >> Procured 49 UH-60M (utility mission) and 24 HH-60M (MEDEVAC mission) helicopters. The M model provides a digitized cockpit, a new engine for improved lift, and range and wide-chord rotor blades. By the end of FY 12, the Army equipped four Assault Helicopter Battalions (AHBs) with the UH-60M.

  >> Procured 50 CH-47F and eight MH-47G (Chinook) aircraft while providing modifications including a loading system, enabling more rapid reconfiguration from cargo to passenger support missions. Continued fielding the CH-47F to the Active and ARNG components, with USAR fielding to begin in FY 14.

  >> Procured 67 Apache AH-64E (Apache Block III) aircraft and provided the existing Block II fleet with modifications that address operationally driven improvements and obsolescence. Improvements: Manned-Unmanned Teaming and Sensors upgrades.

- Funded $48M for RDTE and $35M OPA for Hostile Fire Quick Reaction Capability development, testing, and fielding of the capability in September 2013.

- Funded $26M for the KW helicopter, addressing obsolescence and weight reduction efforts for the aging KW fleet. Also funded the continued research and development of the Cockpit and Sensor Upgrade Program and procurement of long lead items for the first lot of LRIP of OH-58F helicopters.

- Funded $15M in FY 12 the Armed Aerial Scout (AAS) supporting program RDTE.

- Funded $2.9B in FY 12-13 for the Blackhawk helicopter Multi-Year Procurement, procuring 92 UH-60M and 48 HH-60M aircraft. The first year of Multi-Year/Multi-Service VIII contract was FY 12.

- Funded $18.1M in RDTE to support the continued development of the Improved Turbine Engine Program, which is scheduled for a MS A decision in 2013.

- Funded $250M for Lakota in FY 12, of which $244M remains allocated for the Army National Guard. Procured 39 aircraft in FY 12.

- Funded fixed wing aircraft modifications to include Global Air Traffic Management (GATM) upgrades, cockpit upgrades, and mandatory safety upgrades.

- Fielded three new Twin Otters to replace legacy aircraft for the Golden Knights.

- Funded two aircraft for the Army Test and Evaluation Command to replace retiring T-34 aircraft.

- Funded $666M in FY 12 for AH-64E (Apache Block III). The Army remains on schedule to equip the first unit with the AH-64E (Apache Block III) in FY 13.

- Funded $104M in FY 13 for the RQ-7B Shadow, supporting the acquisition of seven TCDL Retrofit Kits and 400 One System Remote Video Terminal (OSRVT) modification kits.

- Funded $25.8M in FY 13 for RQ-11B Raven, procuring 78 gimbaled systems (234 Air Vehicles) and other hardware costs, including ground control stations, remote video terminal, and an initial deployment spares package. The gimbaled payload combines the Electro-optical/Infrared cameras into one payload ball and is a major improvement over the current payloads.

In addition, funding meets unit requests for a virtual training device for system operators.

- Funded $518.1M in FY 13, maximizing the production rate of the MQ-1C Gray Eagle program, procuring 19 MQ-1C aircraft and associated ground support equipment.

- Funded $127M in FY 12 for the Joint Air to Ground Missile (JAGM) which supports the transition of the Army Hellfire missile to a joint missile system. This system replaces the Marine Corps air launched version of the TOW missile and the Navy's Maverick missiles. In addition, funds were applied to the JAGM program restructure which extended the technology development phase.

- Funded $163M in FY 12 for 350 of the Gen3 Electronic Control Units for Common Missile Warning System.

Section III – Key FY 14 Aviation Portfolio Investments:

Fiscal Year 14 Aviation investments total $5.5B ($640M RDTE/$108.5M Procurement of Ammunition, Army (AMMO)/$4.4M MSLS/$4.8B ACFT) and include required capabilities in the reconnaissance, attack, unmanned, utility and cargo, and fixed wing mission profiles. Specific investments in this portfolio include:

- $121M (RDTE) for the Technology Development phase of the Common Infrared Countermeasure (CIRCM) system for Army aviation platforms. CIRCM is a lightweight, low cost, highly reliable laser-based countermeasure system which works in conjunction with Service missile warning systems (i.e. Common Missile Warning System). The program's Full Rate Production decision is scheduled for FY 19.

- $13.1M ($2.3M RDTE/$10.8M ACFT) for RQ-11B Raven, procuring 103 gimbaled payload retrofits and new equipment training (NET).

- $133.9M ($12M RDTE/$121.9M ACFT) for RQ-7B Shadow supporting the acquisition of seven Shadow TCDL Retrofit kits (and associated spare parts), seven launchers, 94 New Mission Computers, six Universal Mission Simulators, and 70 Mobile Directional Antenna System extended range antennas.

- $529.4M ($10.9M RDTE/$518.5M ACFT) procures 15 MQ-1C aircraft and associated ground support equipment.

- $1.3B ($80M RDT&E/$1.2B ACFT) procures 41 UH-60M, 24 HH-60M, funds Improved Turbine Engine Program and UH-60 digital L RDTE efforts, and purchases mission equipment packages.

- $884.2M ($124.8M RDTE/$759.4M ACFT) procures 42 Remanufactured AH-64E (Apache Block III) aircraft and associated modifications to existing AH-64D fleet.

INDIRECT FIRES

SECTION 1— OVERVIEW

To prevail in future operational environments and succeed in a wide range of contingencies, the Army must have a campaign-quality, expeditionary Indirect Fires force that delivers and integrates lethal and non-lethal fires and enables joint commanders in their ability to dominate the operational environment. The Indirect Fires portfolio consists of fire support capabilities in the following four areas: Precision Sensors, Delivery Platforms (Shooters), Munitions, and Field Artillery (FA) C2 Systems. (See figure 8).

To meet the threats of an ever adaptive adversary who employs unconventional tactics, the Army must carefully balance the quantity, quality and management of its equipment. The Indirect Fires portfolio

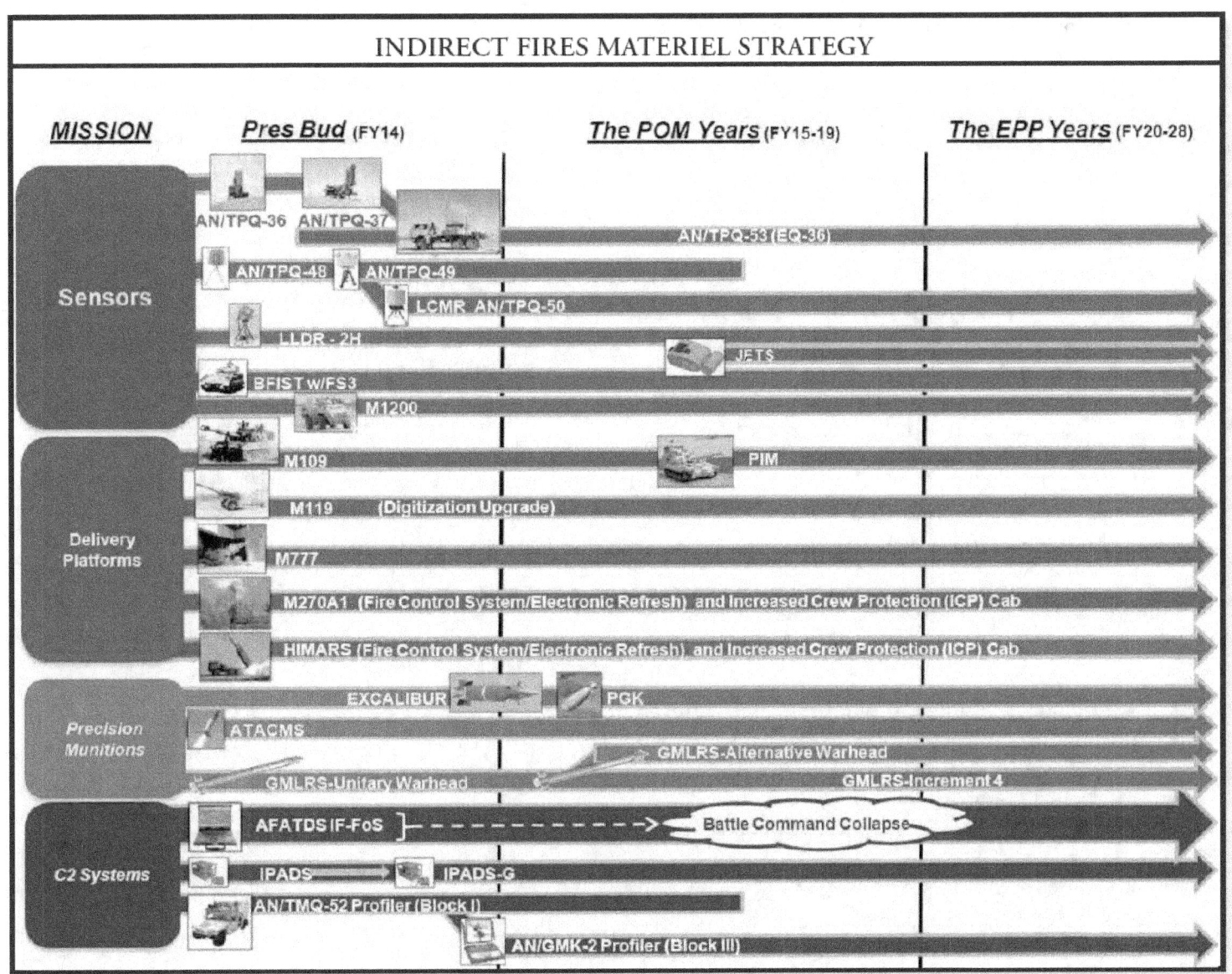

FIGURE 8. Indirect Fires Portfolio (see Acronym Glossary)

includes several types and variants of equipment, which focuses on a vast number of precision and near-precision Indirect Fires missions. To that end, the key strategic objectives for the Indirect Fires portfolio are:

- Improve Precision Targeting capability, especially lightweight, handheld targeting systems.

- Incorporate Joint Fires into procurement planning.

- Develop and procure Precision Munitions supporting Total Army Munitions Requirements.

- Enhance organic Precision Fires capabilities of Infantry Brigade Combat Teams (IBCT).

- Sustain and modernize firing platforms in synchronization with Army modernization plans.

- Support the merging of the command and control program and the Battle Command Network architecture.

- Seek common user interfaces across all Fires launch and radar systems.

- Seek fielding opportunities in providing technologies rapidly to the Soldier.

Section II – Key Indirect Fires Portfolio Accomplishments (FY 12/13):

- Completed fielding and deployed the 12 initial production model Q-53 radar systems in support of Operation New Dawn (OND) and OEF. Fielded 20 additional Q-53 radar systems for units deploying in support of OEF (FY 12).

- Upgraded Firefinder radars (AN/TPQ-36 and AN/TPQ-37) with a new and more reliable radar processor (Q-36 and Q-37) as well as improved power amplifier modules and antenna arrays (Q-37).

- Continued the upgrade of the Lightweight Laser Designator Range-finders (LLDR) supporting the Army directed requirement for increasing precision in employment of Precision Munitions.

- Continued development of the Joint Effects Targeting System (JETS) target location designation system with the technology demonstration phase planned for FY 13.

- Continued improvement of the Q-50 Light-weight Counter Mortar Radar (LCMR) system.

- Completed fielding of High Mobility Artillery Rocket System (HIMARS) launchers (FY 13).

- Continued development of the Multiple Launch Rocket System (MLRS) Improved Armored Cab (IAC) (FY 13).

- Began development of the MLRS launcher Fire Control System–Upgrade (FCS-U) (FY 13).

- Began developmental testing of PIM, addressing long-term sustainability and fires capabilities for the ABCT and conducted Limited User Test in preparation of Milestone C and LRIP decision.

- Completed production of additional M777A2 Howitzers, enhancing organic precision fires capability to IBCTs.

- Began fielding the digitized modifications for the M119A2 105mm Towed Howitzer, addressing responsiveness of fires to support IBCTs.

- Developed and tested Increment 1B of the Excalibur 155mm Precision-Guided Artillery Munition and prepared to begin low-rate Initial Production in 1QFY 13.

- Tested and began procurement of an Urgent

Materiel Release quantity of the Precision Guidance Kit fuse for the 155mm non-precision munitions.

- Will complete fielding of AN/GMK-2, Profiler Meteorological systems, displacing the two vehicle helium balloon meteorological measuring system.

SECTION III – KEY FY 14 INDIRECT FIRES PORTFOLIO INVESTMENTS:

FY 14 Fires (Indirect) investments total $1.6B ($381M RDTE/$353M WTCV/ $428M OPA/$130.1M AMMO/$275.0M MSLS) and include lethal and non-lethal fires and effects such as radars, cannons, launchers, munitions as well as automated enablers. Specific investments in this portfolio include:

- $26M (OPA) develops and procures Lightweight Laser Designator Rangefinder (LLDR) 2H modifications enhancing target location accuracy.

- $21.6M (RDTE) provides RDTE for JETS.

- $30M (WTCV) sustains and improves Bradley Fire Support Team Hardware/ Software modifications with the Fire Support Sensor System (FS3).

- $40.7M (OPA) procures 40 Q-50 LCMR Systems.

- $40M (RDTE) Continue development and testing of the MLRS IAC and the MLRS FCS-U, and develop and test HIMARS software updates.

- $17.7M (MSLS) Begin procurement of MLRS IAC cab and install the HIMARS Enhanced Command and Control (EC2) modification.

Note: FY 14 funding combines MLRS and HIMARS RDTE as well as MLRS Mods and HIMARS Mods MSLS.

- $18.7M (WTCV) develops and procures digitization modifications to M119A2 Howitzer for more responsive fires for IBCTs.

- $67M (AMMO) continues procurement of Excalibur Increment Ib 155mm Precision-Guided Artillery munitions.

- $62M (AMMO) develops and procures Precision Guidance Kit fuses for 155mm non-precision munitions, providing a near-precision capability.

- $80M (RDTE) provides PIM RDTE for continued developmental testing and live fire test. $260.2M (WTCV) funds 18 PIM LRIP vehicle sets.

- $359.9M ($47.2M RDTE / $312.7M OPA) continues procurement of the Q-53 radar system.

AIR AND MISSILE DEFENSE PROTECTION

SECTION 1— OVERVIEW

The Air and Missile Defense (AMD) modernization strategy is driven by a complex and changing operational environment. This strategy requires capabilities that provide defense against advancements in ballistic missiles, manned and unmanned aircraft rockets, artillery, and mortars that threaten friendly forces.

The AMD portfolio consists of required capabilities in the following areas: Ballistic Missile Defense, Counter UAS / Cruise Missile Defense, and Indirect Fire Protection.

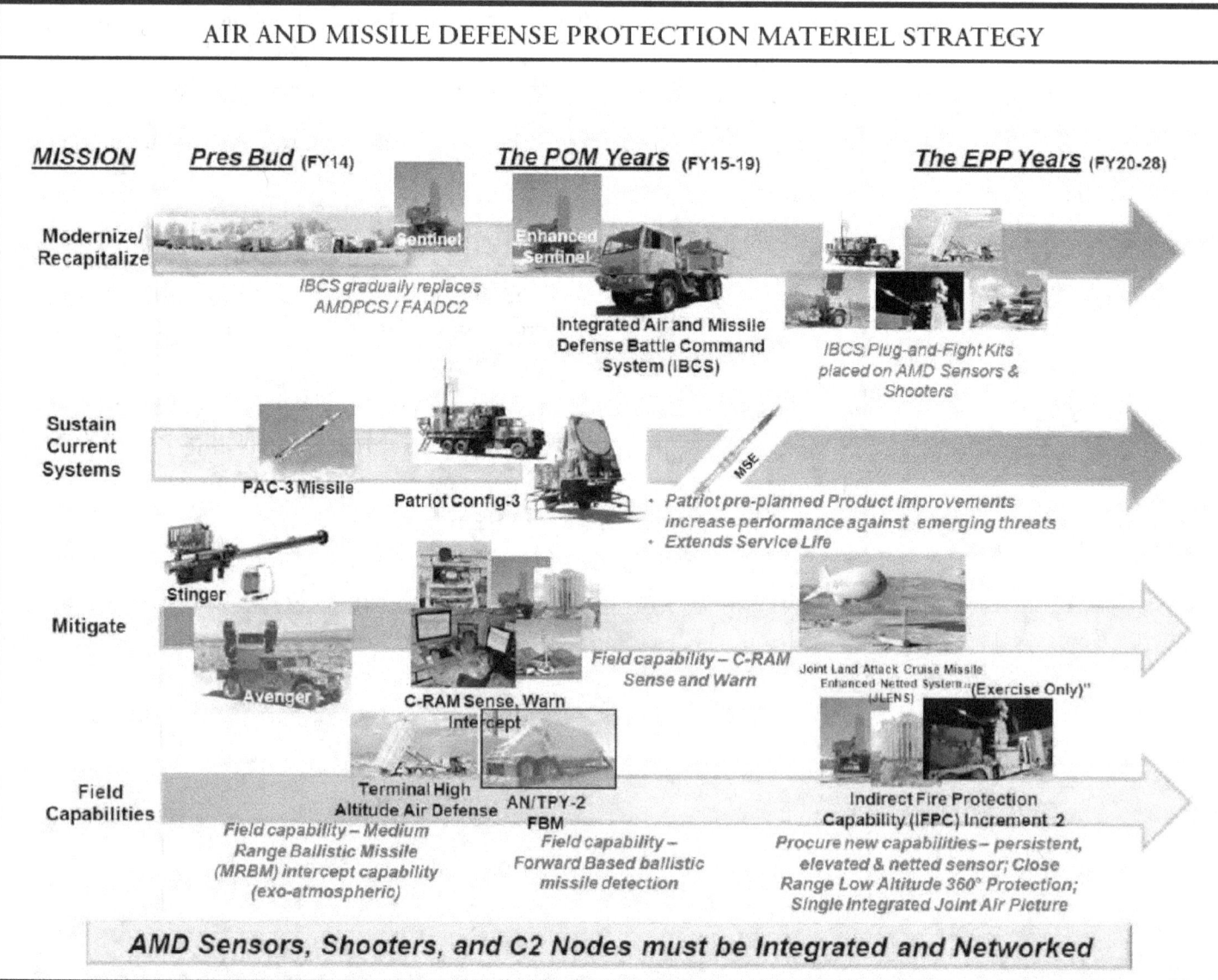

FIGURE 9. *Air and Missile Defense Protection Portfolio (see Acronym Glossary)*

As depicted in figure 9, key imperatives in the AMD portfolio include the common battle manager development recapitalization of current systems, fielding, modernization, and obsolescence improvements, as well as the fielding of new capabilities.

Given the trends and essential capabilities for future Army AMD systems articulated above, the strategic modernization imperatives for AMD are:

Develop and acquire new equipment and improve or recapitalize current systems, remaining relevant and capable of closing capability gaps and achieving dominance in core capabilities.

- Increase capabilities to counter rockets, artillery, and mortars.

- Conduct a comprehensive, pre-planned product improvement effort, incrementally modernizing and upgrading performance of the Patriot system.

- Conduct Service Life Extension Program (SLEP) and capability improvements on Stinger missiles, increasing their counter-UAS capabilities.

Close capability gaps, extend useful life of existing equipment.

- Develop, acquire, and field a common battle manager/C2 node for all Army AMD forces. This manager is modular, open, net-centric and operationally scalable.

- Fuse/integrate the air picture with fire control quality data.

- Integrate sensors and weapons on the network through "plug and fight."

- Enable Joint Integrated Fire Control across U.S. Army, Navy and Air Force platforms.

Procure systems capable of meeting the threats of today and tomorrow.

- Develop and procure a next generation Indirect Fire Protection Capability (IFPC) to providing effective, full spectrum protection for joint and maneuver forces.

Provide the Soldier with the quantity and type of equipment required, enabling training, preparation, and employment for mission successes.

- Field Terminal High-Altitude Area Defense (THAAD), a new capability providing a medium-range ballistic missile intercept capability.

- Field the Patriot Missile Segment Enhancement (MSE), the latest variant of the Patriot Advanced Capability (PAC-3) missile and, in conjunction with ground system hardware and software upgrades, provides a critical increase in capability.

SECTION II – KEY AIR AND MISSILE DEFENSE PROTECTION PORTFOLIO ACCOMPLISHMENTS (FY 12/13):

- Upgraded the last of three older Patriot units to PAC-3 capability (launcher upgrades continue).

- Completed fielding of Patriot Grow the Army battalion # 15.

- Continued reset of Patriot equipment operating in the United States Central Command (USCENTCOM) area of responsibility, completing two battalion sets by July 2012.

- Continued providing Rockets, Artillery, and Mortar (RAM) sense and warn capabilities in support of Operation Enduring Freedom at 24 sites in Afghanistan.

- Began fielding RAM warn suites to Army BCTs.

- Funded the activities necessary to begin fielding of two active component Avenger battalions into Indirect Fire Protection Capability (IFPC)/ Avenger battalions.

- Transitioned RAM sense and warn capabilities to Office of Security Cooperation - Iraq and Department of State sites in Iraq as part of support for United States Mission - Iraq. Withdrew and reset 22 Counter-Rockets, Artillery, and Mortars (C-RAM) intercept systems previously in preparation to fielding the newly established IFPC/Avenger Composite Battalions in the first quarter of FY 14.

- Conducted reset of 20 Air Defense and Airspace Management (ADAM) Cells and 18 Forward Area Air Defense Command and Control (FAAD C2) shelters.

- Fielded three Air and Missile Defense Planning and Control Systems to Patriot Battalions (Composite).

- Conducted reset of 39 ADAM Cells and 33 FAAD C2 shelters.

- Transitioned the Air and Missile Defense Work Station to the Windows operating system.

- Completed Sensor C2 and Sentinel Radar fielding to all division headquarters.

- Completed modernization of six basic Sentinel radars to Improved Sentinel radars in the National Capital Region (NCR). These radars have enhanced target range and classification as well as radar reliability / supportability via improved electronics.

- Completed developmental testing of the Sentinel Radar IFPC, enhancing fratricide prevention and improving integration into the C-RAM Command and Control architecture. Completed software release to USCENTCOM/

OEF and NCR in July 2011 and to the remainder of the fleet in September 2011.

- Validated the acquisition strategy to procure 431 Army Integrated Air and Missile Defense (AIAMD) Battle Command System Engagement Operation Centers in line with the strategy to transition all current and future AMD capabilities to one mission command architecture for AMD battle management.

Section III – Key FY 14 Air and Missile Defense Protection Portfolio Investments:

The FY 14 Air and Missile Defense investments total $1.9B ($723M RDTE/$174M OPA/0 AMMO/$844M MSLS/$123M OMA) and include developing and acquiring new equipment and improving or recapitalizing current systems. These investments offer increased C-RAM capabilities, improve and increase Patriot missile inventory, conduct pre-planned product improvement efforts of the Patriot system, conduct Service Life Extension Program and capability improvements on Stinger missiles, close capability gaps, extend the useful life of existing equipment, and field additional Terminal High-Altitude Area Defense batteries. Specific investments in this portfolio include:

- $98.5M (RDTE): $64M to complete Joint Land Attack Cruise Missile Defense Elevated Netted Sensor (JLENS) EMD scheduled test phase and $34.5M to support a single orbit deployment exercise in FY 14.

- $70M (RDTE) supports ongoing modeling, simulation and testing required to assess current and emerging threats, continue Patriot software upgrades, and continue missile system integration.

- $609M ($68.8M RDTE/$540.4M MSLS) begins procurement of MSE missiles and procures additional Patriot Enhanced Launcher Electronic System launcher upgrades. It also continues upgrading Patriot (including modern man stations, radar digital processor), and provides critical software upgrades to address advanced Tactical Ballistic Missiles, electronic attacks, and communications upgrades.

- $365M (RDTE) continues AIAMD development and enables initial deliveries by FY 16.

- $12M (OPA) supports continued fielding of RAM Warn to Army BCTs.

- $43M (OPA) supports fielding of C-RAM Interceptors to the AC IFPC/Avenger Battalions and completes improvements to RAM Warn architecture based on operational lessons learned.

- $1.6M (RDTE) begins SLEP and integrates capability improvements to field 850 Stinger missiles by FY 15.

Force Protection

Section I— Overview

The Force Protection modernization plan procures Assured Mobility; Force Protection; and selected Chemical, Biological, Radiological, and Nuclear (CBRN) defense equipment that is effective and affordable. This equipment provides American Soldiers with the highest levels of force protection, civil affairs/military information support operations (CA/MISO) capabilities, and enhanced engineering abilities consistent with the functional application of these materiel solutions in support of assigned missions. Current modernization efforts include procuring new and improved materiel solutions that enhance our capabilities in current and future years. Figures 10-11 display a selected array of mature capabilities as projected from current, near, and extended term perspectives.

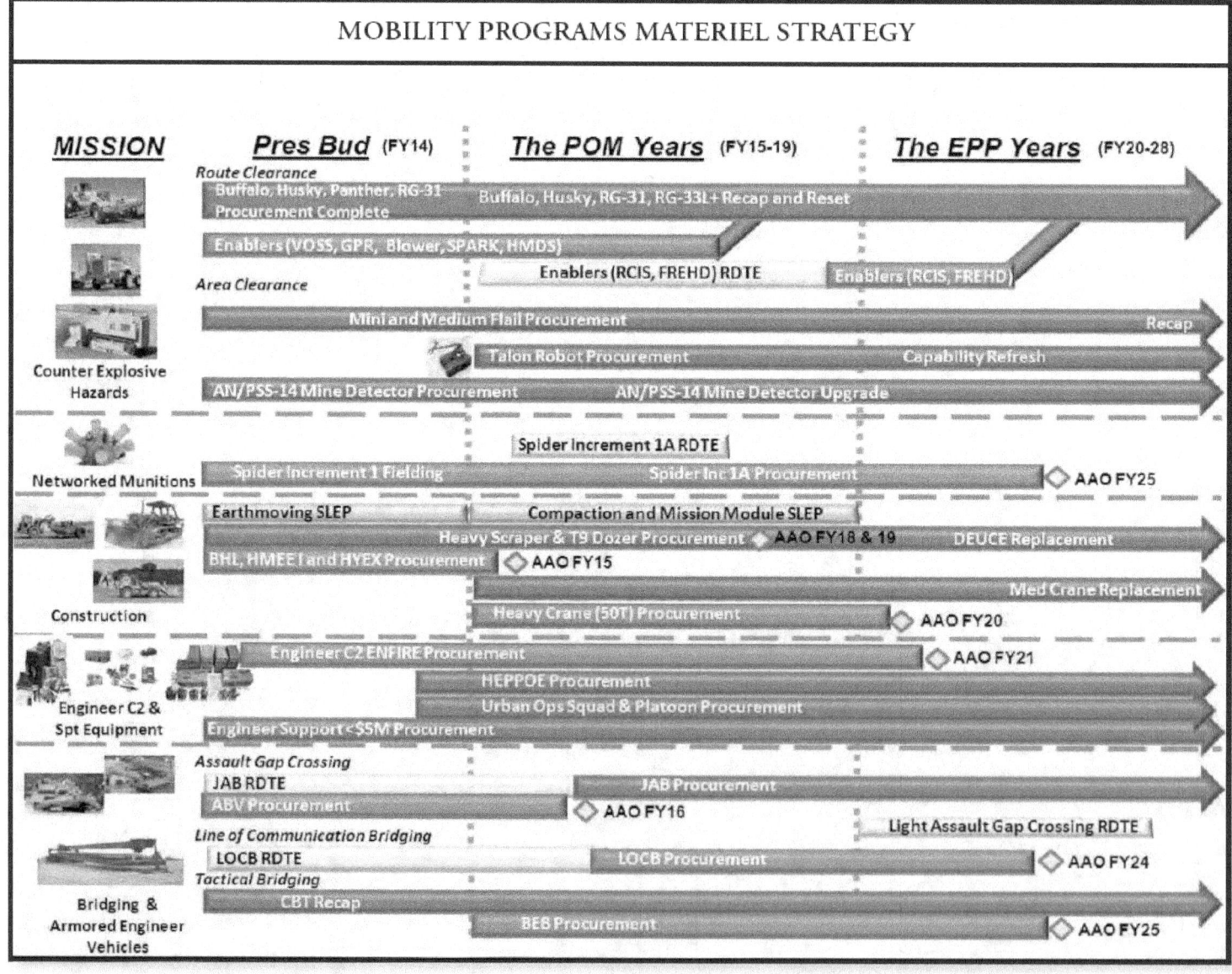

FIGURE 10. Force Protection Portfolio: Mobility Programs (see Acronym Glossary)

Section II – Key Force Protection Portfolio Accomplishments (FY 12/13):

- Fielded 170 Mine Protected Clearance Vehicles Buffalos, 334 Vehicle Mounted Mine Detection Huskies, and 456 AN/PSS-14 Handheld Mine Detectors in support of Route Clearance units.

- Fielded 83 Hydraulic Excavators, 340 Medium Dozers, and 30 Heavy Scrapers; fielding

continues through FY 14. Procured 19 Assault Breacher Vehicles (ABV) to support fielding three ABCTs.

- Provided 446 Urban Operations Sets to platoons and squads enabling assured mobility in the urban environment.

- Provided 97 Hydraulic, Electric, Pneumatic, Petroleum Operated Equipment (HEPPOE) to support missions by clearing buildings for repair and construction, clearing areas around

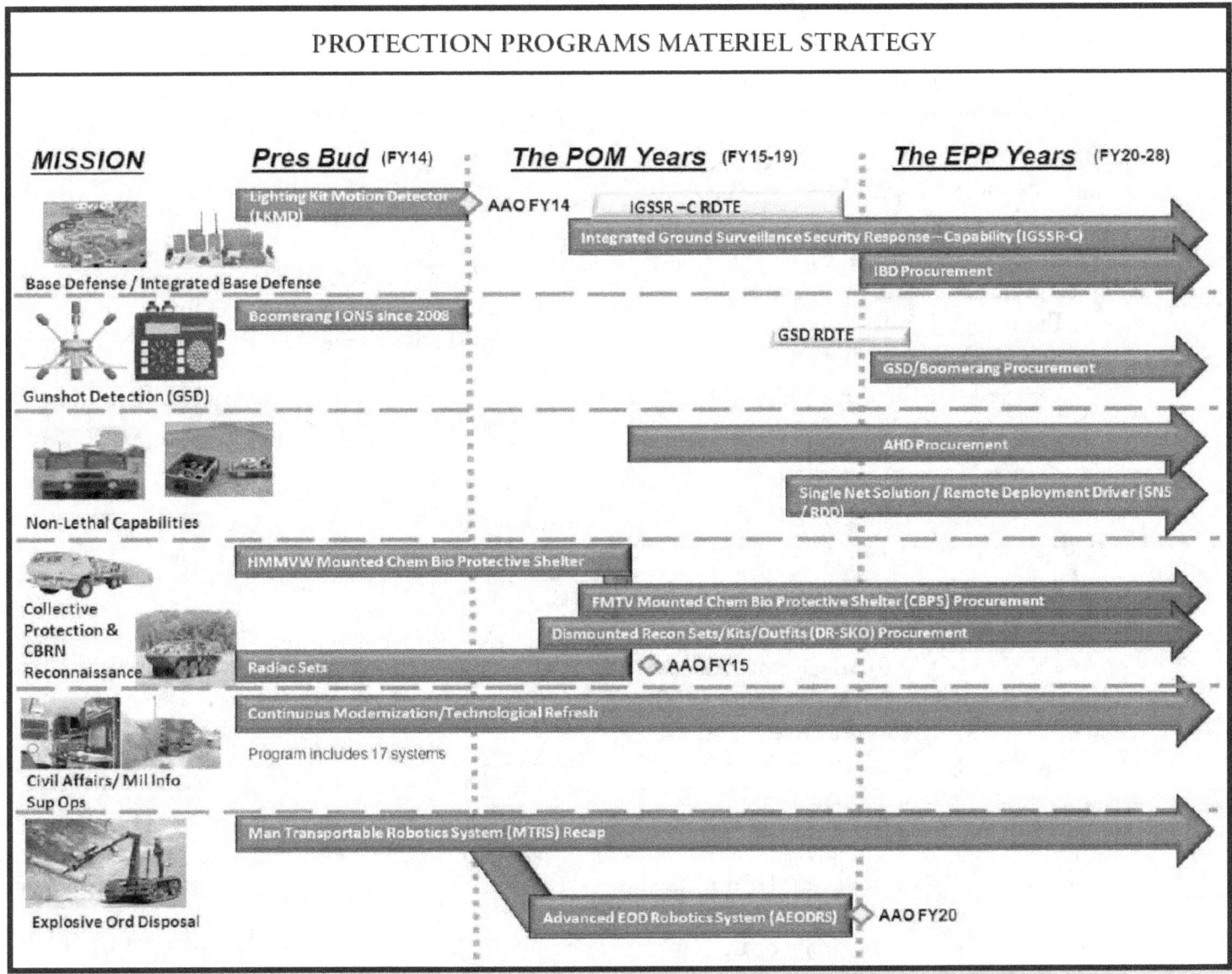

PROTECTION PROGRAMS MATERIEL STRATEGY

FIGURE 11. Force Protection Portfolio: Other Protection Programs (see Acronym Glossary)

road construction, port openings, and any other areas that require operations in an urban area.

- Procured 20 ABVs, 30 Heavy Scrapers, 171 T9 Dozers, 60 Water Distributors, and 221 Instrument Set, Reconnaissance, and Surveying (ENFIRE) sets for three ABCTs in FY 12.

- Recapitalized over 200 Route Clearance and Explosive Ordnance Disposal (EOD) vehicles into their program of record configuration in FY 12.

- Procured 3,200 Launched Electrode Stun Device and 2,546 Battlefield Anti-Intrusion System (BAIS) completing the Army investment into these programs.

- Procured 7,038 Joint Combat Identification Marking System (JCIMS) kits for United States Forces Korea, Combat Training Centers, and Army Pre-positioned Sets. The complete JCIMS hardware package includes Combat Identification Panels, Thermal ID Panels, and Infra Red Lights. The panels provide a combat identification marking capability to enable friendly platform and Soldiers to identify each other on the battlefield to minimize fratricide incidents and to enhance combat effectiveness. The current approved Army Acquisition Objective for JCIMS is 148,035. JCIMS will complete fielding in FY 13 and transition to sustainment.

- Fielded the Joint Service Aircrew Mask (JSAM) Apache (MPU-6(V)/P) to 16 Combat Aviation Brigades. The JSAM Apache (MPU-6(V)/P) replaces the legacy M48 Protective Mask. The new mask is compatible with the Joint Service Aircrew Ensemble and the Apache Integrated Helmet and Display Sighting System.

- Fielded 42 additional Biological Integrated Detection Systems (BIDS). These systems complete the final three platoons of the 307th Chemical Company (21 systems) and one platoon for the 308th Chemical Company (7 systems) in Federal Emergency Management Agency region IX, and added two platoons of capability to the 365th Chemical Company (14 systems) in Salt Lake City, Utah. BIDS is a fully deployable, critical dual use system that can be used for contingency operations as well as homeland defense.

SECTION III – KEY FY 14 FORCE PROTECTION PORTFOLIO INVESTMENTS:

The FY 14 Force Protection investments totaling $716.4M ($105.4M RDTE/$611M OPA) ensure Soldiers are protected from multitude of battlefield and homeland security hazards. Specific investments in this portfolio include:

- $107.3M (OPA) funds recapitalization of over 222 Route Clearance and EOD vehicles and 48 Self Protect Adaptive Roller Kits into program of record configuration for fielding; upgrades 547 AN/PSS-14 Handheld Mine Detectors to the new Revision 6; provides $76M in RDTE for the next generation of standoff detection, neutralization, and clearance systems.

- $63M (WTCV) procures 14 ABV systems for two ABCTs enabling rapid breaching, proofing and marking of full width lanes through complex obstacles and minefields.

- $63.1M (OPA) modernizes dry and wet gap bridging with the Improved Ribbon Bridge (IRB), a float bridge; and Dry Support Bridge.

- $221.2M (OPA) modernizes 52 Heavy Scrapers, 13 Engineer Mission Module Water Distributors, 84 Medium Dozers, 109 Hydraulic Excavators, and 19 Heavy Cranes.

- $44M (OPA) modernizes 59 HEPPOE, 230 Urban Operations Sets, and some under $5M Line items.

- $19.3 (OPA) procures 212 Instrument Set, Reconnaissance and Surveying Systems to Engineer formations across the Army.

- $20.9M (OPA) procures 8,362 EOD Equipment systems. The program includes 8 systems comprised of the Advanced Explosive Ordnance Disposal Robotic Systems and associated equipment providing EOD technicians with a rapid, reliable, and secure means for identifying and disarming EOD munitions.

- $61.1M (OPA) procures 528 Civil Affairs / Military Information Support Operations (CA/MISO) systems. The program includes 17 systems providing essential command and control, communications, computers and intelligence (C4I) capabilities for CA/MISO General Purpose Forces.

- $8.9M (OPA) procures 774 BAIS; provides early seismic/acoustic warning, intrusion detection, and characterization of approaching ground intrusion threats.

- $27.2M (RDTE) develops improved controller for Spider Increment IA system

- $2M (WTCV) develops Joint Assault Bridge technology modernizing the obsolete Armored Vehicle Launched Bridge fleet.

- $410K (RDTE) funds EOD Equipment RDTE providing increased standoff distances for IED-Defeat missions, particularly for vehicle-borne IEDs.

Sustainment (Transport)

Section 1— Overview

The Sustainment (Transport) Portfolio consists of Tactical Wheeled Vehicles (TWV) and Watercraft fleets.

The TWV fleet includes Light, Medium, and Heavy Tactical Vehicles with associated trailers and the MRAP family of vehicles. TWVs are employed in many combat service support mission roles such as armament carrier, recon, convoy operations, troop and cargo transport, CASEVAC, and C2. The vision of an Army truck has evolved tremendously in a short period of time. Simple unprotected motorized transportation platforms for people and equipment are practical in the training base, but do not meet current threats in

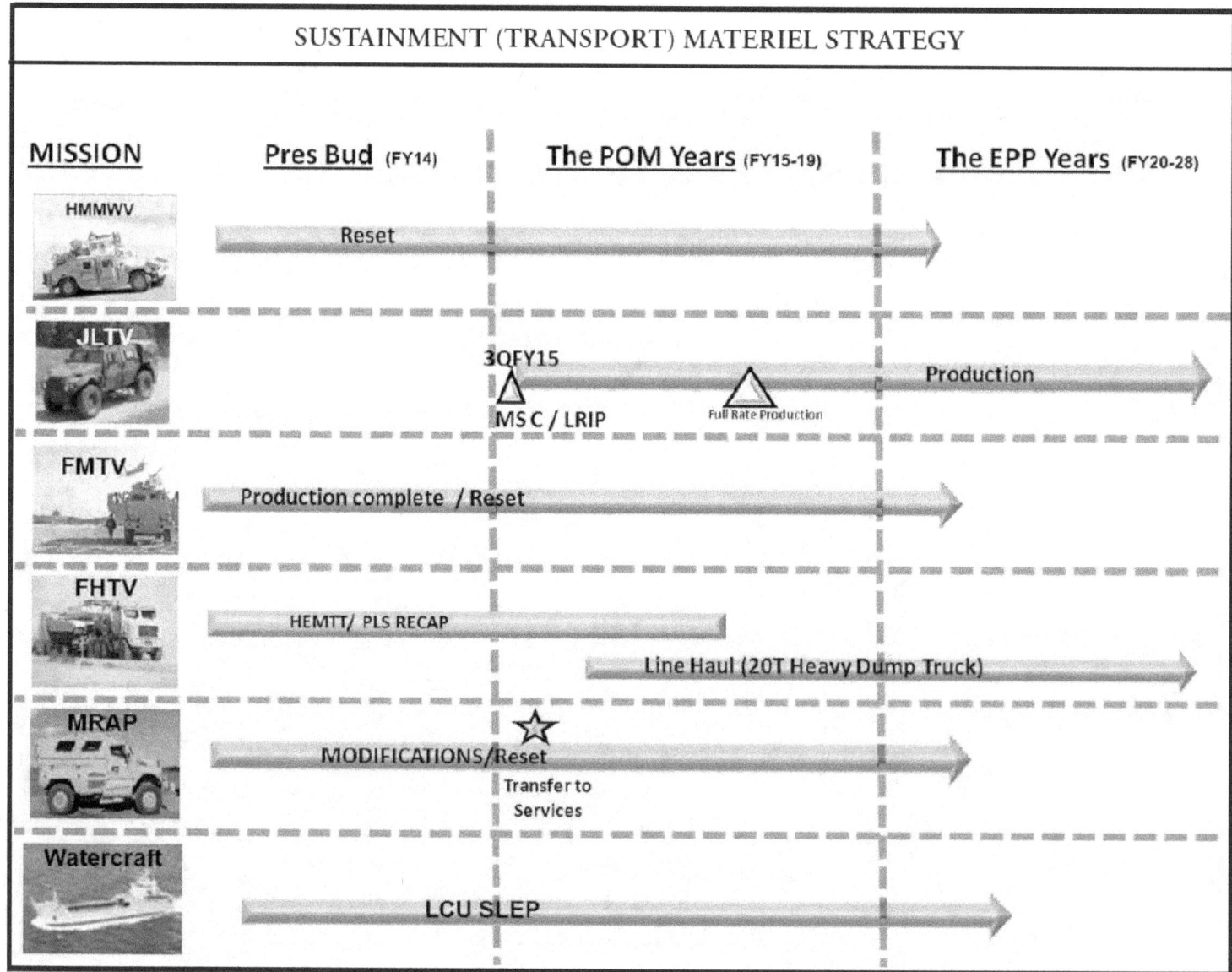

FIGURE 12. Sustainment (Transport) Portfolio (see Acronym Glossary)

deployed environments. Trucks must be armored or armor capable and have the additional capacity and power to carry the additional weight and power required to protect personnel and support a wide variety of Command, Control, Communications and Computers, and Intelligence, Surveillance and Reconnaissance (C4ISR) equipment and other mission equipment such as mine rollers and the CROWS to remain relevant on today's multi-spectrum battlefields.

The Watercraft fleet consists of 118 platforms and systems that are described in four categories: Command and Control, Causeway Systems, Landing Craft and Floating Craft. Command and Control systems, such as the Harbormaster Command and Control Center and Landing Craft Mechanized Mod 2, provide C2 of port assets, visibility and input to the Common Operating Picture, and cargo tracking. Causeway Systems, such as Roll-on/roll-off Discharge Facility, Causeway Ferry, Warping Tug, and Floating Causeway, allow throughput in constrained draft and beach gradient conditions. The causeways provide the critical linkage between strategic shipping and shore discharge. Landing Craft, such as Logistics Support Vessel, Landing Craft Utility, and Landing Craft Mechanized Mod 1, provide intra-theater lift of time sensitive, mission critical personnel, and materiel in support of ground forces. The Floating Craft, such as Small and Large Tug Boats and Barge Derrick, provide heavy lift, towing, repair, and salvage capability.

As depicted in figure 12, key objectives and decision points in the Tactical Wheeled portfolio include:

- Fully funding Joint Light Tactical Vehicle (JLTV) Family of Vehicles in the EMD Phase. Three vendors (AM General, Lockheed-martin, and Oshkosh) were awarded contracts to provide 22 each full-up prototypes for the EMD phase for

testing and evaluation. Hardwire, a non-EMD vendor, has expressed its intent to compete for the EMD phase.

- Modernize the Family of Heavy Expanded Mobility Tactical Truck (HEMTT) and Palletized Loading System (PLS) through recapitalization.

- Family of Medium Tactical Vehicle (FMTV) fleet production ends in FY 14.

- Integration of the MRAP fleet as an Army program of record in FY 13.

- Sustainment and modernization of the current Landing Craft Utility (LCU) fleet through Service Life Extension Program (SLEP) and C4ISR upgrades. Continue development/integration of Army Watercraft Strategy force protection.

SECTION II – KEY SUSTAINMENT (TRANSPORT) PORTFOLIO ACCOMPLISHMENTS (FY 12/13):

- In FY 12, fielded in excess of 1,912 MRAP All Terrain Vehicles, 186 MRAP Wreckers in support of OEF.

- In FY 12, completed the depot-level repair (reset) of approximately 250 Heavy Tactical Wheeled Vehicles (TWVs) and recapitalized 976 HEMTTs and PLSs.

- In FY 12, the Army completed the SLEP of the Logistical Support Vessel (LSV); in FY 13 begin SLEP of the LCU vessel.

- In FY 13, the Army will field in excess of 10,900 FMTV trucks and trailers.

- In FY 12, the Army fielded in excess of 3,094 Family of Heavy Tactical Vehicles (FHTV) trucks and trailers.

- In FY 13, the Army will procure over 1,004 trucks and 1,538 trailers within the FMTV fleet and procure 713 armor protection kits. The FHTV fleet will procure 618 trucks, trailers, and other associated systems and recapitalize 77 HEMTTs and PLSs and procure 249 armor protection kits.

- In FY 13, JLTV program will continue in its second year in the EMD phase. The three EMD vendors as well as EMD non-vendors are expected to have completed their prototypes by the end of the third quarter.

Section III – Key FY 14 Sustainment (Transport) Portfolio Investments:

The FY 14 Sustainment (Transport) Portfolio investments total $575M ($110M RDTE/ $464M OPA).

- In FY 14, $84.2M (RDTE) funding has been allocated for the JLTV program. The program will continue in the EMD phase conducting testing and evaluation.

- $4M (OPA) to procure 67 Light Engineer Utility Trailer for Vertical Engineer Companies.

- $14.1M (OPA) to procure 70 Enhanced Container Handling Units and 150 PLS trailers.

- $224M (OPA) to procure 780 FMTV trucks and 57 trailers. The program reaches completion in FY 14.

- $39.5M (OPA) to recapitalize 77 HEMTTs into armor capable configuration.

- $44.3M (OPA) to recapitalize 74 PLSs into armor capable configuration.

- $51.3M (OPA) to procure 746 armor kits for FMTVs and FHTVs.

- $72.2M (OPA) procures SLEP for 2 x LCU 2000's; and buys 16 sets of C4ISR for Army Watercraft Systems.

SUSTAINMENT

SECTION 1— OVERVIEW

The Sustainment portfolio consists of multiple systems providing essential enabling equipment. These systems include: Joint Precision Airdrop Systems (JPADS), Modular Fuel System-Tank Rack Module (MFS-TRM), Load Handling System Compatible Water Tank Rack System (HIPPO), Assault Kitchen, Multi-Temperature Refrigerated Container System (MTRCS), 5K Light Capacity Rough Terrain Forklift (LCRTF), Metal Working and Machining Shop Set (MWMSS), Armament Repair Shop Set (ARSS), Human Remains Transfer Case Improved (HRTC2), Next Generation Automatic Test System (NGATS), Maintenance Support Device (MSD) Version 3, Calibration Sets, Medical Field Systems (MFS), Medical Communication for Combat Casualty Care (MC4), and Force Provider (FP) Base Camp Operational Energy Efficiency Modification (Mod) Kits.

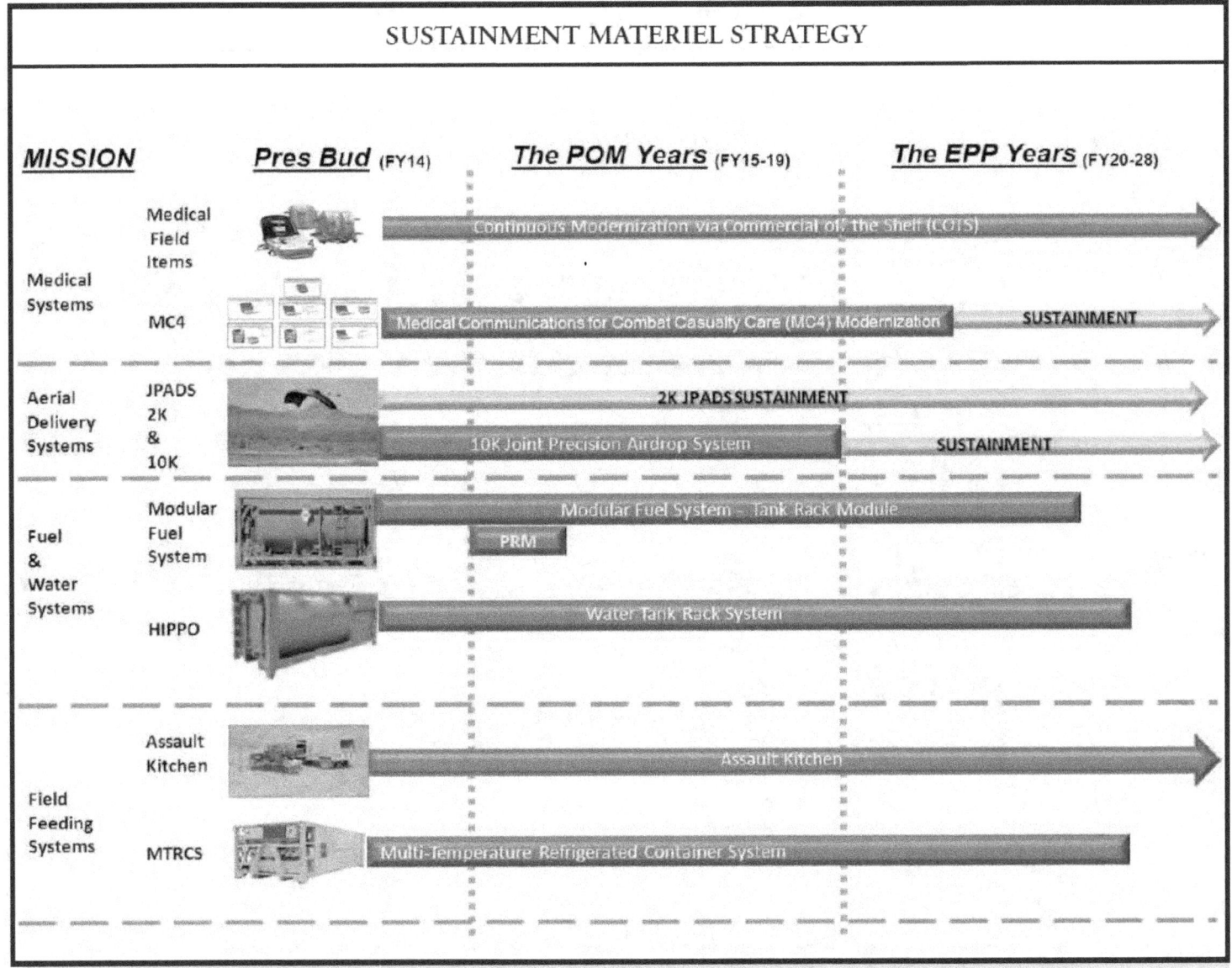

FIGURE 13. Sustainment Portfolio Modernization (see Acronym Glossary)

Section II – Key Sustainment Portfolio Accomplishments (FY 12/13):

- Fielded 55 each 10,000 pound JPADS. The 10K JPADS provide rapid, precise, high altitude delivery capabilities to forces without the use of ground transportation.

- Fielded 174 MTRCS to BCTs increasing storage capabilities and enhancing quality of life for units/detachments operating in remote locations.

- Fielded 244 HIPPO systems providing a capability which receives stores and issues large quantities of potable water anywhere in the theater of operations. The HIPPO replaces the Forward Area Water Point Supply System.

- Fielded 440 each ATLAS II Forklifts to various units such as BCTs, CABs, Ordnance Units, and Transportation Units. Its primary mission includes loading and unloading 20 foot ANSI/ISO containers and handing loads up to

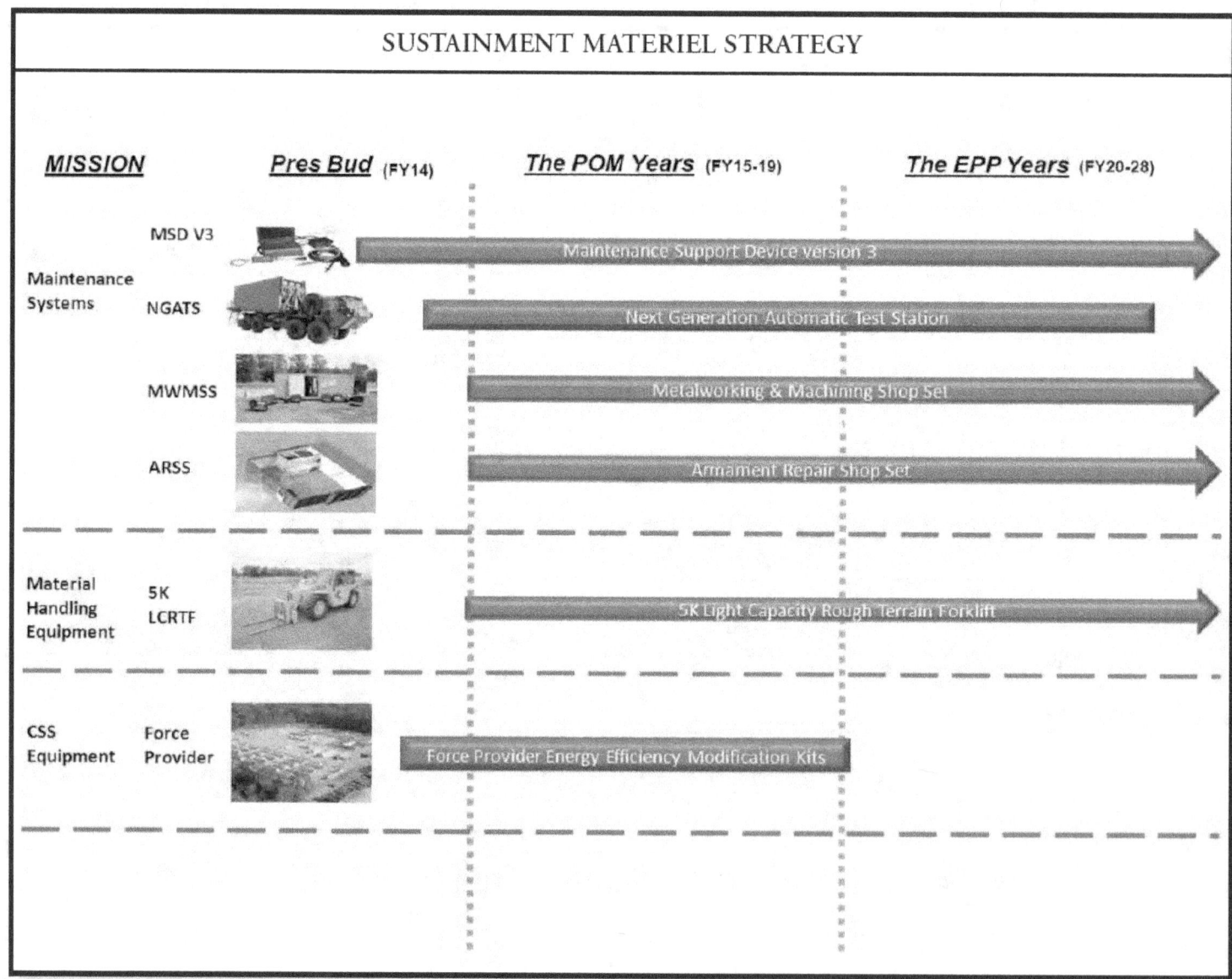

FIGURE 14. Sustainment Portfolio Modernization (see Acronym Glossary)

10,000 lbs with 48 inch load centers (Air Force 463L pallets).

- Fielded 1,002 Maintenance Support Devices (MSD-V3) to Special Operations Forces and BCTs at Ft. Stewart and Ft. Bragg to improve maintenance diagnostic capability for ground equipment.

Section III – Key FY 14 Sustainment Portfolio Investments:

The FY 14 Sustainment investments total $518M ($86M RDTE/$344M OPA/$88M OMA) for support programs and include fuel and water systems, load handling systems, airdrop systems, tool sets, medical systems, and other combat enablers. Specific investments in this portfolio include:

- $57.4M (OPA) and $54.3M (OMA) procures 3,258 medical systems and 88 medical evaluation mission enhancement packages for HH-60 helicopters. OMA procures 1,325 medical equipment sets that provide health service support for Soldiers on the battle field with current standards of care.

- $22.8M (OPA) procures 1,396 of pieces of the Medical Communication for Combat Casualty Care that supports medical information system, enabling lifelong electronic medical records, streamlined medical logistics, and enhanced situational awareness for Army operational forces.

- $34M (OPA) procures 306 Tank Rack Modules providing a mobile fuel storage capability for 12 BCTs.

- $34M (OPA) procures 2,000 MSDs V3 replacing obsolete test sets in 16 BCTs.

- $33.5M (OPA) procures 13 NGATS replacing legacy Direct Support Electrical System Test Sets and legacy Base Shop Test Facility in five BCTs.

- $22.6M (OPA) procures 156 MTRCS providing rapid refrigerated transport and storage of Class I items for 11 BCTs.

- $26.6M (OPA) procures 306 HIPPO replacing obsolete Semi-Trailer Mounted Fabric Tanks (SMFT) and Forward Area Water Point Supply Systems (FAWPSS) in seven BCTs.

- $8M (OPA) procures three calibration sets replacing obsolete calibration sets in three BCTs.

- $9.5M (OPA) procures 61 each 10K JPADS in support of joint precision aerial delivery operations conducted in numerous theaters of operations/ training missions.

- $5.7M (OPA) procures 60 each 5,000 pound forklifts replacing legacy 4,000 pound forklifts throughout the Army.

- $5M (OPA) procures 84 Assault Kitchens (AK) replacing legacy field fielding systems in Special Forces detachments and BCTs.

- $15M (OPA) procures 26 MWMSS replacing 24 legacy systems.

- $4M (OPA) procures nine ARSS in three BCTs.

- $3M (OPA) procures 342 Human Remains Transfer Case Improved replacing legacy Human Remains Transfer Case used to preserve human remains in transit.

- $34.2M (OPA) procures 30 FP Modification Kits for FP Reset/FP production to modernize FP Base Camp Modules and provide a totally integrated Resource and Energy Efficiency capability that reduces fuel consumption by up to 50 percent, water consumption by up to 90 percent and waste by 80 percent.

SCIENCE AND TECHNOLOGY PROGRAM

SCIENCE AND TECHNOLOGY PROGRAM

The Army Science and Technology (S&T) investments support Army modernization goals to develop and field affordable equipment in a rapidly changing technological environment. The Army's S&T mission is to enable Soldiers to dominate the battlefield today and tomorrow by focusing resources, which include a qualified team of S&T personnel and adaptive organizations, to innovate, mature, demonstrate and transition technologies that address Army challenges. The U.S. Army depends on its S&T Program to research, develop, and demonstrate high pay-off technological solutions to hard problems faced by Soldiers in worldwide operations with diverse threats. Army S&T delivers timely technology that addresses the Army's challenges, while developing technology solutions that Soldiers will need in the future to prevent, shape, and win future conflicts in an uncertain, complex world. We seek to invest our S&T where we must (i.e., Army-specific areas), and leverage from industry, international partners, other government investments, etc. where we can.

S&T projects are planned and executed collaboratively with the Army's 22 laboratories and Research, Development, and Engineering Centers (RDECs) and Soldiers/leaders who employ warfighting capabilities represented by TRADOC. The Army Capabilities Integration Center (ARCIC), a field operating agency supporting HQ, Training and Doctrine Command (TRADOC), manages the Army's architecture of the future to ensure that the Soldier's requirements are integrated and understood. Where appropriate, partnerships are developed among the Services, Department of Defense (DoD) laboratories, industry, academia, and international partners. The Army's S&T investments reflect a balanced approach to far-term, basic research for discovery and understanding of phenomena (Research, Development, Test & Engineering (RDT&E) Budget Activity (BA) 1); mid-term, applied research for laboratory concept demonstrations to develop and evaluate the feasibility and practicality of proposed solutions (RDT&E BA 2); and near-term, advanced technology demonstrations of subsystems and components in relevant environments outside the laboratory (RDT&E BA 3) that support efforts such as Operational Need Statements or initiatives undertaken by the Rapid Equipping Force. In addition, we have established an Army S&T and Acquisition partnership that invests a portion of the Army's RDT&E BA 4 funding (Advanced Component Development and Prototypes) against high potential technologies/sub-systems and further matures them for demonstration in relevant environments and operational scenarios. It also seeks to support the competitive prototyping of technologies and systems earlier in the acquisition life cycle, ensuring competition while reducing technological risk to Army programs of record. In addition, TRADOC Centers of Excellence ensure that promising capabilities from emerging technologies are transitioned to the Soldier through enabling concepts, programs of record, or insertion into the Total Force. This investment, upon which we will continue to build, is showing progress in creating a more seamless path for transition out of S&T and into programs of record.

The Army S&T program is organized into six investment portfolios that address challenges across four Army-wide capability areas (Soldier; Air; Ground; Command, Control, Communications, and Intelligence (C3I)) and two S&T enabling areas (Basic Research and Innovation Enablers):

• The Soldier Portfolio includes sub-portfolios in Human Dimension, Human Systems Integration, Survivability, Individual and Small Unit Equipment, and Combat Casualty Care. The Soldier Portfolio executes innovative S&T programs that increase the effectiveness, health, and reliability of the human component of the total Army allowing for rapid dominance in increasingly complex environments across a diverse range of operations.

- The Air Portfolio aims to be the global leader in providing game-changing range, payloads, speed, survivability, and lethality to maintain U.S. technical superiority and combat overmatch for vertical lift aviation systems. It includes sub-portfolios in the areas of Platform Design & Structures; Engines & Drive trains; Aircraft Occupant Survivability; Maintenance & Sustainability; Rotors & Vehicle Management; Aircraft Weapons & Sensors; and Unmanned & Optionally Manned Systems.

- The Ground Portfolio includes sub-portfolios for: Survivability, Weapons, Ground Platforms (manned and unmanned), and Mobility and Countermobility to provide our Soldiers with overmatch of offensive and defensive capabilities in weapons and military vehicles.

- The C3I Portfolio has a vision to provide Soldiers at the tactical edge with trusted and responsive sensors, communications, and information adaptable in dynamic, austere environments to support battlefield operations and non-kinetic warfare. Its sub-portfolio includes: Communications, Mission Command, Sensors, and Intelligence/Electronic Warfare.

- The Innovation Enablers Portfolio includes the Environmental Quality & Installation and High Performance Computing sub-portfolios. The management of the DoD High Performance Computing Modernization Program devolved from the Office of the Secretary of Defense to the Army in Fiscal Year 2012 (FY 12). This program supports all Services and DoD Agencies, provides advanced computational capabilities as a solution of first resort to explore and evaluate new theories; reduces time and cost of acquiring weapons systems; and enables real-time calculations in support of military operations.

- Underpinning all of the Army S&T efforts is a strong Basic Research program that builds an agile and adaptive foundation of technical understanding so that the Army is able to respond to future threats. The Basic Research Portfolio includes the following sub-portfolios: Human Centric, Information Centric, Material Centric, Platform Centric, and Enrichment Initiatives. Investing wisely in people with innovative ideas is our best approach to catching unexpected discoveries for the "Army of the Future." To create the environment for discovery, it is important to continue making smart investments in basic and applied research, especially in Army-unique areas.

The following are examples of major efforts within the S&T Portfolio with near term products:

- The Warrior Injury Assessment Manikin (WIAMan) Program is an effort to design a new instrumented test manikin that provides enhanced capability to measure the blast waves and acceleration changes that occur on a vehicle occupant during vehicle under body blast events. The WIAMan Program will design a test tool that replicates human injury and allows injury prediction by pairing test asset development with medical research. The project will evaluate skeletal injuries to occupants during such events, and will develop skeletal injury criteria to be used during combat vehicle Live Fire Test Events to improve vehicle design and Soldier survivability. The first blast manikin prototypes will be available in FY 15.

- The Extended Area Protection and Survivability (EAPS) Program supports the development of a robust counter-rocket, artillery, and mortar capability that provides 360-degree protection against asymmetric, simultaneous RAM attacks.

The EAPS program is developing gun and missile-based technologies and demonstrating system concepts supporting these requirements. Demonstrated technology designs include those for components and fully integrated missile interceptors, a course-corrected projectile, their respective Fire Control Sensors, and Technical Fire Controls. Upon transition, technologies will have demonstrated successful flight-tested intercepts against single and multiple incoming RAM threats. An integrated demonstration of the capability to defeat both single and multiple, near-simultaneous RAM targets in live-fire testing is planned for FY 14.

- The Occupant Centric – Force Protection Program improves force protection and mitigates Soldier injury due to underbody IED and mine blast, vehicle rollover, and vehicle crash events. This design philosophy considers the Soldier first, integrates occupant protection technologies, and builds the vehicle to support Soldiers and their mission. To this end, Army S&T is developing an occupant centric survivability concept design demonstrator, as well as platform-specific demonstrators. The program is also publishing standards for occupant centric design guidelines, test procedures, and safety specifications, as well as improving modeling and simulation capabilities.

- The Deployable Force Protection (DFP) Program is transitioning mature technology to Soldier's today by leveraging the expertise of a wide variety of the Army's labs and centers, as well as S&T efforts throughout the Services and DoD. These S&T solutions drive toward resilient, low-logistics, lightweight, easily transportable, and minimal manpower products that readily scale and integrate with other base defense systems. This allows for enhanced protection capabilities, while leaving Soldiers with more time to perform their mission.

The program provides Soldiers operating at forward operating bases (FOBs) with protection capabilities such as overhead cover and structures that incorporate advanced blast and ballistic protection. Other technologies include, but are not limited to, sensors; blast and ballistic materials; remotely operated and precision active protection systems; communications; denial and deception; and enablers to achieve situational awareness and understanding. The program employs an Adaptive Red Team (ART) to identify vulnerabilities of potential deployable force protection technologies that could threaten their successful fielding, use, and operational effectiveness in the hands of Soldiers. ART combines the Technical Support and Operational Analysis live experiment quarterly venues, ART research and development, and the red team, intelligence support components. The ART realistic, adaptable environment brings together Soldiers, industry, and technical personnel to assess and improve technologies.

- The Air Portfolio is engaged in a range of ongoing applied research and technology development efforts, including support for the planned Future Vertical Lift (FVL) acquisition program. The Joint Multi-Role (JMR) Technology Demonstrator (TD) is the S&T program designed to develop next-generation aircraft concepts that demonstrate vastly improved range, speed, survivability, and payload capacity to meet the operational capabilities required of future aviation systems. These concepts will inform the design and development of the planned FVL acquisition program, and reduce technical risk by evaluating critical technologies early. By partnering with industry and academia, Army S&T is specifically working on engineering new aviation systems able to sustain speeds in excess of 170 knots; achieve an overall mission range greater than 800 kilometers (out and back) un-refueled; and hover with a full combat load under high density altitude conditions, while also addressing operational and sustainment costs. Plans for additional FVL technologies include enhanced vehicle and occupant survivability; internal weapons carriage; next-generation sensors for target detection and identification; a common, open systems architecture for on-board avionics; manned-unmanned teaming ability; and shipboard compatibility. The JMR TD seeks to begin designs for several demonstrator aircraft in 2013 and will conduct first flights in 2017 as a series of steps toward developing the next-generation fleet of vertical lift aircraft by 2030.

- Within the C3I portfolio, Army S&T is providing solutions to improve C2, situational awareness, and dynamic communications, while maintaining appropriate military security not found in commercial devices. For example, the Actionable Intelligence technology initiative is developing and maturing tools to collect and transform Intelligence data into timely and relevant situational understanding that reduces tactical surprise for Soldiers at the company-level and below. It focuses on Operations/Intelligence convergence, automated Company Intelligence Support Team (CoIST) tools, and sensor exploitation at the tactical edge to provide equipped units with tactical information overmatch currently only available to higher echelons. The effort is structured into four thrust areas that will be completed in FY 14-15: Proactive Data Services; CoIST Fusion Services; Analyst Collaborative Tools; and Overwatch Sensor Grid. Capabilities and technologies include lighter and more effective sensor payloads (for improved minefield, IED, and threat detection); improved urban terrain and combat identification sensors (through structure sensing, friend/foe disambiguation); and a tool suite that utilizes the Distributed Common Ground System - Army standard architecture to perform threat projections and provide near-real-time tips and cues to the squad.

- Army S&T is also exploring emerging technologies that may result in future critical (and affordable) capabilities for assured communications and persistent ISR, and that may be useful in future Anti-Access/Area Denial environments. One such area of Army S&T investment is in nano-satellite technology to augment or provide redundant capabilities to the tactical Soldier. In partnership with USSOUTHCOM, the USAF Space Test Program (STP), and the Office of the Secretary of Defense, the Nano Satellite-3 Joint Capability Technology Demonstration (JCTD), will demonstrate beyond line-of-sight communications and data exfiltration via three nanosatellites in a Low Earth Orbit constellation. In partnership with USPACOM, the Department of Defense, and the USAF STP, the Kestrel Eye JCTD will demonstrate a proof-of-concept to provide overhead Joint Photographic Experts Group (JPEG) imagery directly to tactical commanders in response to their Tasking, Collection, Processing, Exploitation, and Dissemination process via a constellation of four small satellites.

As the Army S&T Program continues to identify and harvest technologies suitable for transition to our Force, we aim to remain ever vigilant of potential and emerging threats. We are implementing a strategic approach to modernization that includes an awareness of existing and potential gaps; an understanding of emerging threats; knowledge of state-of-the-art commercial, academic, and government research; as well as a clear understanding of competing needs for limited resources. Army S&T will sharpen its research efforts to focus upon those core capabilities it needs to sustain, while identifying promising or disruptive technologies able to change the existing paradigms of understanding. Ultimately, the focus remains upon Soldiers; Army

S&T consistently seeks new avenues to increase the Soldier's capability and ensure their technological superiority today, tomorrow, and decades from now. The Army S&T mission is not complete until the right technologies provide superior, overmatch capability for our Soldiers.

For FY 14, the Army has dedicated more than $2B to its S&T Program, all of which is aligned with the Army's needs and priorities: $437M in RDT&E BA 1 (Basic Research), $886M in RDT&E BA 2 (Applied Research), $882M in RDT&E BA 3 (Advanced Technology Demonstrations) and $636M in RDT&E BA4 (Advanced Component Development and Prototypes).

Capability Fielding
and Distribution

CAPABILITY FIELDING AND DISTRIBUTION

The Army Equipping Reuse Working Group (AERWG) and the Army Equipping Strategy are key to ensuring Soldiers have what they need when they need it.

The AERWG is a semi-annual event that brings representatives of all the equipment stakeholders (Army Commands, Army Service Component Commands, Direct Reporting Units, the Army National Guard, and the Army Reserves) together to review the Army's equipping posture and policies, discuss issues, and synchronize equipment distribution.

The Army Equipping Strategy (http://www.g8.army.mil/pdf/AES2012_lq.pdf) describes the ends, ways, and means the Army will use to ensure Soldiers and units have the right equipment in the quantities needed to accomplish assigned missions in support of combatant commander requirements. It establishes goals and metrics for achieving an affordable balance between requirements and resources. The strategy describes how equipment and capabilities, provided by the Army Equipment Modernization Plan, are distributed and placed into a unit to synchronize it with its assigned mission. It addresses the rotational and non-rotational Operational Force and the Generating Force. The Strategy is a dynamic and flexible document that addresses the divergent needs and requirements for all components.

Although the strategy must be flexible enough to meet current needs, it is founded upon the basic principle that Soldiers will have what they need, when needed. To this end, the strategy is based on three lines of operation applied.

Unit-Based Equipping. The Army's equipping goal is to ensure that Soldiers and units always have the equipment they need to execute assigned missions. It measures success using a series of equipping goals established in an Army Force Generation (ARFORGEN)-based model. The Army equips Active and Reserve Component units incrementally, based on personnel strengths, training requirements, and the amount of time before their next deployment. All units have at least 90 percent of their authorized equipment in time to train adequately prior to deployment.

The Army is examining alternative equipping strategies because of OPTEMPO changes caused by the return of forces and equipment from Iraq, economically driven resource constraints, and the reduction of forces in Afghanistan. Once codified, these will be incorporated in the Army's equipping strategy.

The Unit-Based Equipping line of operation also includes tailoring equipment distributions to manage shortages better and maximize capabilities; maintaining the Generating Force and RC Critical Dual Use equipping levels to no less than 80 percent.

Managing Friction. Friction is the equipment that is being used to meet other critical Army requirements such as filling equipment sets, going through Reset, or in transit over strategic distances rather than filling unit requirements. Success in Managing the Friction Line is measured by how well the Army can see its own equipment inventories and make informed management decisions about how to allocate that inventory to build Army readiness. Friction is a drain on valuable resources and it increases the complexity of equipping units. One way the Army has reduced friction is by establishing a single Lead Materiel Integrator (LMI) under the Army Materiel Command. The LMI mission is to synchronize the distribution and redistribution of materiel in accordance with DoD and Army directives and priorities.

Building Long Term Readiness. The Army will continue to focus on Army management policies and structure to bring resources, resourcing processes, requirements validation, and priorities into better synchronization with cyclic equipping readiness requirements. Some of the methods the Army is using to build long-term readiness as it manages risk in a fiscally-constrained era are optimizing equipment distribution via Lead Material Integration processes, ensuring property accountability and requirements documents accurately reflect equipping status, updating the readiness reporting system, and examining the relevance of long-standing equipping programs and policies.

The second aspect of ensuring Soldiers have the equipment they need is the AERWG. The goal of the AERWG is to ensure Soldiers are equipped for the current fight and for future contingencies. The AERWG combines knowledgeable, experienced equippers with representatives from all stakeholders across the Army in a focused venue that ensures Combatant Commanders have the most capably equipped units the Army can provide, while allowing participants an opportunity to address a wide range of key Army equipping concerns.

The AERWG enables a holistic view of the Army's equipping posture, policies and issues. It is a venue in which stakeholders (equipment providers and using units) can refine equipping plans. The results of each AERWG are briefed to the senior Army leadership. During this brief the HQDA DCS, G-8, provides an analysis of the Army equipping situation and identifies issues that affect readiness.

The conference provides two key outputs. The first is the information sharing that comes from special topic working sessions. These sessions sustain communications across the community of stakeholders on strategic issues affecting Army equipping policy and posture. They provide the commands with a forum to receive updates and address questions or concerns on current and evolving issues that impact our collective equipping efforts. The second is a refined distribution plan for the next 21 months. The plan ensures Soldiers get the right equipment at the right place at the right time.

LEAD MATERIEL INTEGRATOR

The Army Materiel Command (AMC) is the Army's Lead Materiel Integrator (LMI). The command was assigned the mission to increase efficiency, eliminate redundancy, increase cost savings, and improve materiel readiness. The LMI approach to Army materiel management combines transparency of decisions, collaboration among all materiel stakeholders, a strategic view of all materiel requirements and sources of supply over time, and consolidation of multiple authoritative inputs in one place, yielding a synchronized materiel distribution and redistribution process that optimizes supply against demand.

The Army Sustainment Command, AMC's executive agent for LMI, uses an automated decision support tool (DST) to help it formulate equipping recommendations to the field. The DST provides increased asset visibility using data from the Army's authoritative materiel data repository, the Logistics Information Warehouse (LIW). The LIW and the DST optimize supply against demand, allowing the Army to distribute and redistribute materiel with unprecedented speed and precision. This results in increased efficiencies, elimination of redundancies, cost savings and improved materiel readiness.

CONCLUSION

The United States Army is the world's decisive land force. Our Soldiers and formations must be equipped, enabled, and prepared to operate in complex and uncertain battlefields, supported by precise information overmatch capabilities delivered to the right place and at the right time. The FY 14 President's Budget balances the current and future needs, provides the basis for an affordable equipping strategy over time, and takes into account Army requirements and priorities.

The Army Equipment Modernization Plan 2014 describes the Research, Development, and Acquisition (RDA) portion of the Fiscal Year 2014 President's Budget request, which reflects the Army's Priority materiel programs and identifies the critical capabilities to succeed in the full range of missions, while maintaining a decisive advantage over any adversary.

The Army will continue to develop and field a versatile and tailorable mix of equipment that is affordable and enables Soldiers to succeed in the full range of missions today and tomorrow. This approach will balance equipment modernization with end strength and readiness to mitigate risk to our Soldiers and programs.

As we re-balance the Army from the previous decade of conflict to reflect the future fiscal, operational, and technical environments in which we will operate, we will continue to make affordable, sustainable, and cost-effective decisions to provide our Soldiers, the regional Combatant Commanders, and our Nation the necessary ground force options and capabilities to meet today's and tomorrow's challenges.

Acronym Glossary

Acronym Glossary

AAS	Armed Aerial Scout
ABCS	Army Battle Command Systems
ABV	Assault Breach Vehicle
AC	Active Component
ACFT	Aviation Procurement, Army
ADAM	Air Defense Airspace Management (Cell)
AEMS	Army Equipment Modernization Strategy
AERWG	Army Equipping Reuse Working Group
AFATDS	Advanced Field Artillery Tactical Data System
AGPU	Aviation Ground Power Unit
AGSE	Aviation Ground Support Equipment
AHB	Assault Helicopter Battalions
AHD	Acoustic Hailing Device
AIAMD	Army Integrated Air and Missile Defense
AIM SA	Abrams integrated management situational awareness
AK	Assault Kitchen
AMC	Army Materiel Command
AMD	Air and Missile Defense
AMDPCS	Air and Missile Defense Planning and Control System
AMDWS	Air and Missile Defense Work Station
AMMPS	Advanced Medium Mobile Power Source
AMPV	Armored Multi-purpose Vehicle
ANSI/ISO	American National Standards Institute / International Organization for Standardization
APG	Aerial Precision Geolocation
ARB	Attack Reconnaissance Battalion
ARCIC	Army Capabilities Integration Center
ARFORGEN	Army Force Generation
ARL	Airborne Reconnaissance Low
ARNG	Army National Guard
ARSS	Armament Repair Shop Set
ART	Adaptive Red Team
ASE	Aircraft Survivability Equipment
ATC	Air Traffic Control
ATIRCM	Advanced Threat Infrared Countermeasures
ATNAVICS	Air Traffic Navigation, Integration and Coordination
B	Billions
BAIS	Battlefield Anti-Intrusion System
BCT	Brigade Combat Team
BEB	Bridge Erection Boat
B-FIST	Bradley Fire Support Team (Vehicle)

BfSB	Battlefield Surveillance Brigade
BHL	Backhoe Loader
BIDS	Biological Integrated Detection System
C2	Command and Control
C2 / SA	Command and Control / Situational Awareness
C3I	Command, Control, Communications, Intelligence
C4I	Command, Control, Communications, Computers and Intelligence
C4ISR	Command, Control, Communications, Computers, Intelligence, Surveillance and Reconnaissance
CA/MISO	Civil Affairs and Military Information Support Operations
CAB	Combat Aviation Brigade
CASEVAC	Casualty Evacuation
CASUP	Cockpit And Sensor Upgrade Program
CBPS	Chemical Biological Protective Shelter
CBRN	Chemical, Biological, Radiological and Nuclear
CBT	Common Bridge Transporter
CDTE	Counter Defilade Target Engagement
CE	Computing Environment
CEH	Counter Explosive Hazards
CENTCOM	United States Central Command
CHARCS	Counterintelligence and Human Intelligence Automated Reporting and Collection System
CI	Counterintelligence
CIRCM	Common Infrared Countermeasures
COE	Common Operating Environments
CoIST	Company Intelligence Support Team
COMINT	Communications Intelligence
COMSEC	Communication Security
COP	Common Operating Picture
COTS	Commercial Off the Shelf
CPOF	Command Post of the Future
CPCE	Command Post Computing Environment
C-RAM	Counter-Rockets, Artillery and Mortars
CROWS	Common Remotely Operated Weapon System
CS	Combat Support; or Capability Set
CSB	Configuration Steering Board
CSP	Common Sensor Payload
CSS	Combat Service Support
DAB	Defense Acquisition Board
DCGS-A	Distributed Common Ground System - Army
DDL	Digital Data Link

www.g8.army.mil

Acronym Glossary

DEUCE	Deployable Universal Combat Earthmover
DFP	Deployable Force Protection
DHCP	Digital Host Communication Protocol
DMTI	Digital Moving Targeting Indicator
DoD	Department of Defense
DOMEX	Document and Media Exploitation
DR-SKO	Dismounted Recon – Sets, Kits, Outfits
DSB	Dry Support Bridge
DST	Decision Support Tool
DVH	Double V Hull
EAB	Echelons Above Brigade
EAPS	Extended Area Protection and Survivability
EC2	Enhanced Command and Control
ECP	Engineering Change Proposal
ECS	Engagement Control Station
ECU	Environmental Control Unit
EMARSS	Enhanced Medium Altitude Reconnaissance Surveillance System
EMD	Engineering and Manufacturing Development
EN	Engineers
ENFIRE	Instrument Set, Reconnaissance and Surveying
EO/IR/LD	Electro-optical/Infrared/Laser Designator
EOD	Explosive Ordnance Disposal
EPA	Environmental Protection Agency
EPLRS	Enhanced Position Location and Reporting System (Radio)
EPP	Extended Planning Period
ERMP	Extended Range Multi-Purpose (Unmanned Aerial System) (Gray Eagle)
ESA	Enhanced Situational Awareness
ESB	Expeditionary Signal Battalion
FA	Field Artillery
FAAD C2	Forward Area Air Defense Command and Control
FAWPSS	Forward Area Water Point Supply System
FCS-U	Fire Control System – Upgrade
FDD	Full Deployment Decision
FHTV	Family of Heavy Tactical Vehicles
FISINT	Foreign Instrument Signal Intelligence
FMTV	Family of Medium Tactical Vehicles
FMV	Full Motion Video
FOB	Forward Operating Base
FOV	Family of Vehicles
FP	Force Provider

FREHD	Forward Reconnaissance and Explosive Hazard Detection
FS3	Fire Support Sensor System
FUA	Fixed Wing Utility Aircraft
FUE	First Unit Equipped
FVL	Future Vertical Lift
FW	Fixed Wing
FY	Fiscal Year
GATM	Global Air Traffic Management
GBS	Global Broadcast System
GCSS-A	Global Command Support System – Army
GCV	Ground Combat Vehicle
GEOINT	Geospatial Intelligence
GMLRS	Guided Multiple Launch Rocket System
GMTI	Ground Moving Target Indicator
GPR	Ground Penetrating Radar
GRCS	Guardrail Common Sensor
GSD	Gunshot Detection
HBC	High Band COMINT
HBCT	Heavy Brigade Combat Team
HD	High Definition
HEMTT	Heavy Expanded Mobility Tactical Truck
HEMTT-LHS	Heavy Expanded Mobility Tactical Truck-Load Handling System
HEPPOE	Hydraulic, Electric, Pneumatic, Petroleum Operated Equipment
HIMARS	High Mobility Artillery Rocket System
HIPPO	Load Handling System Compatible Water Tank Rack System
HMDS	Husky Mounted Detection System
HMEE	High Mobility Engineer Excavator
HMMWV	High Mobility Multipurpose Wheeled Vehicle
HMS	Handheld, Manpack and Small Form Fit (radios)
HQ	Headquarters
HRTC2	Human Remains Transfer Case Improved
HUMINT	Human Intelligence
HYEX	Hydraulic Excavator
IAC	Improved Armored Cab
IBCS	Integrated Air and Missile Defense – Battle Command System
IBCT	Infantry Brigade Combat Team
IBD	Integrated Base Defense
ICD	Initial Capabilities Document
ICP	Increased Crew Protection
IED	Improvised Explosive Device

www.g8.army.mil

IEWS	Integrated Electronic Warfare System
IF-FoS	Indirect Fire Family of Systems
IFPC	Indirect Fire Protection Capability
IFV	Infantry Fighting Vehicle
IGSSR-C	Integrated Ground Surveillance Security Response – Capability
IOTE	Initial Operational Test and Evaluation
IP	Internet Protocol
IPADS	Improved Position and Azimuth Determining System
IPADS-G	Improved Position and Azimuth Determining System integrated with Global Positioning Satellite
IRB	Improved Ribbon Bridge
ISO	In support of
ISR	Intelligence Surveillance and Reconnaissance
ITAS	Improved Target Acquisition System
JAGM	Joint Air to Ground Missile
JBC-P	Joint Battle Command-Platform
JCIMS	Joint Combat Identification Marking System
JCR	Joint Capabilities Release
JCTD	Joint Capability Technology Demonstration
JETS	Joint Effects Targeting System
JIIM	Joint, Interagency, Intergovernmental, and Multi-National
JLENS	Joint Land Attack Cruise Missile Defense Elevated Netted Sensor
JLTV	Joint Light Tactical Vehicle
JMR	Joint Multi-Role
JPADS	Joint Precision Airdrop System
JPEG	Joint Photographic Experts Group
JSAM	Joint Service Aircrew Mask
JTRS	Joint Tactical Radio Systems
JWICS	Joint Worldwide Intelligence Communications System
KW	Kiowa Warrior
LCMR	Lightweight Counter-Mortar Radar
LCRTF	Light Capability Rough Terrain Forklift
LCU	Landing Craft Utility
LET	Light Equipment Transport
LHS	Load Handling System
LKMD	Lighting Kit Motion Detector
LLDR	Lightweight Laser Designator Rangefinder
LMI	Lead Materiel Integrator
LOCB	Line of Communication Bridging
LRIP	Low Rate Initial Production

LSV	Logistic Support Vessel
LWN	LandWarNet
M	Millions
MC	Mission Command
MC4	Medical Communications for Combat Casualty Care
MCE	Mounted Computing Environment
MEDEVAC	Medical Evacuation
MFLTS	Machine Foreign Language Translation System
MFS	Modular Fuel System; Medical Field Systems
MFS-TRM	Modular Fuel System Tank Rack Module
MLRS	Multiple Launch Rocket System
MNVR	Mid-tier Networking Vehicular Radio
MOTS	Mobile Tower System
MP	Man Pack
MPCV	Mine Protected Clearance Vehicles
MRAP	Mine Resistant Ambush Protected (vehicle)
MRBM	Medium Range Ballistic Missile
MS A	Milestone A (acquisition milestone)
MS B	Milestone B (acquisition milestone)
MS C	Milestone C (acquisition milestone)
MSD	Maintenance Support Device
MSE	Missile Segment Enhancement
MSLS	Missile Procurement, Army
MTRCS	Multi-Temperature Refrigerated Container System
MTRS	Man Transportable Robotic System
MUM	Manned - Unmanned Teaming
MWMSS	Metal Working and Machine Shop Set
NBCRV	Nuclear Biological, Chemical Reconnaissance Vehicle
NCR	National Capital Region
NET	New Equipment Training
NetOps	Network Operations
Nett	Not an acronym - honors World War II Medal of Honor recipient Colonel Robert B. Nett
NGATS	Next Generation Automatic Test System
NIE	Network Integration Evaluation
NW	Nett Warrior
OCO	Overseas Contingency Operations
ODS-SA	Operation Desert Storm-Situational Awareness (Abrams Tank variant)
OEF	Operation Enduring Freedom
OIF	Operation Iraqi Freedom
OMA	Operations & Maintenance, Army

Acronym Glossary

OND	Operation New Dawn
OPA	Other Procurement, Army
OSRVT	One System Remote Video Terminal
OTV	Outer Tactical Vest
PAC	Patriot Advanced Capability
PB	President's Budget
PED	Processing, Exploitation and Dissemination
PGK	Precision Guidance Kit
PIM	Paladin Integrated Management
PLS	Palletized Load System
POM	Program Objective Memorandum
POR	Program of Record
PRM	Pump Rack Module
QCB	Quick-Change Barrel
R&D	Research and Development
RAM	Rockets, Artillery and Mortars; also Reliability, Availability and Maintainability
RC	Reserve Component
RCIS	Route Clearance Interrogation System
RDA	Research, Development and Acquisition
RDEC	Research, Development, and Engineering Center
RDTE	Research, Development, Test and Evaluation
RR	Rifleman Radio
RSTA	Reconnaissance, Surveillance and Target Acquisition
S&T	Science and Technology
SAR	Synthetic-Aperture Radar
SATCOM	Satellite Communications
SECM	Shop Equipment Contact Maintenance
SEP	System Enhancement Package
SFAAT	Security Forces Assistance Advisory Teams
SICPS	Standard Integrated Command Post System
SIGINT	Signals Intelligence
SLEP	Service Life Extension Program
SMET	Squad Multi-purpose Equipment Transport
SMFT	Semi-trailer Mounted Fabric Tank
SNS/RDD	Single Net Solution / Remote Deployment Driver
SOF	Special Operations Forces
STARLite	Small Tactical Radar Lightweight
STEP	Strategic-Tactical Entry Points
STORM	Small Tactical Optical Rifle-Mounted (STORM)
STP	USA Space Test Program

SWaP-C	Size, Weight, Power and Cooling
TAIS	Tactical Airspace Integration Systems
TBC	Tactical Battle Command
TCDL	Tactical Common Data Link
TD	Technology Demonstration
TENCAP	Tactical Exploitation of National Capabilities
THAAD	Terminal High Altitude Area Defense
TOW	Tube-Launched, Optically-Tracked, Wire-Guided
TPE	Theater Provided Equipment
TSP	Tactical SIGINT Payload
TWV	Tactical Wheeled Vehicles
U.S.	United States
UAS	Unmanned Aircraft System
USAR	United States Army Reserve
VBIED	Vehicle Borne IED
VOSS	Vehicle Optics Sensor System
VSAT	Very Small Aperture Terminal
VSP	Village Stability Platforms
WIAMan	Warrior Injury Assessment Maniken
WIN-T	Warfighter Information Network – Tactical
WTCV	Weapons and Tracked Combat Vehicles

* Details on major Army acquisition programs can be found in the 2013 Army Weapon Systems handbook at: http://armyalt.va.newsmemory.com/wsh.php

www.ingramcontent.com/pod-product-compliance
Lightning Source LLC
Chambersburg PA
CBHW080514290526
45790CB00006B/2164